On This Spirit Walk

Henrietta Mann
Anita Phillips

Native American Comprehensive Plan
The United Methodist Church

Copyright Information

The copyright for materials in this book is retained by the individual authors. It is the philosophical and political position of the Native American Comprehensive Plan of the United Methodist Church that it is vital for indigenous authors to retain control of their work, particularly when the work contains stories from the lives of individuals, families, communities and nations which are unique and sacred to that context. Should there be a request for permission to reprint or use any portion of this book in a setting other than this volume, the request should be directed to the Native American Comprehensive Plan who will, in turn, contact the author(s). Such requests may be directed to: NACP, 928 North York Street, Suite 2, Muskogee, Oklahoma 74403 or nacomp@prodigy.net.

Dedication

This book is dedicated to the tribes and indigenous nations of the world. May the words of this book offer truth, hope and inspiration unto seven generations.

The initial printing of *On This Spirit Walk* is made possible through the contribution of the General Commission on Christian Unity and Interreligious Concerns. The Native American Comprehensive Plan gratefully acknowledges this gift.

Contents

A Note from the Authors/Editors

We have been blessed by the opportunity to write and edit this book. First of all, our meeting one another has been a gift. In the many conversations we have shared there has been a subtext of two Native American women coming to know and appreciate one another. We had not met prior to this project, but there is no doubt we will continue our relationship far beyond its completion.

So much of what we and all the contributing authors shared comes from our personal experience of lives walked in these particular moccasins. The stories and oral tradition information are much more than so many words on a page. We trust our readers to treat what we have written with appreciation and respect. If you notice, the copyright remains in the name of each author. This is a philosophical-political statement about peoples of oral tradition. The content of our writing includes stories and anecdotes from our families, communities, tribes, and peoples. We closely guard the sanctity of these stories and ask that should you want to use parts of our writing in other ways (outside the purpose of a small group curriculum) that you contact the Native American Comprehensive Plan, a sponsoring organization for this book.

We both pray that the contents of *On This Spirit Walk* will honor and celebrate the Great Mystery who has brought us all together through the power of both the spoken and written word. We share it with hope, joy and expectation of great things our Creator God will do through its reading.

Dr. Henrietta Mann
Weatherford, Oklahoma

Rev. Anita Phillips
Park Hill, Oklahoma

Introduction

The idea for this book originated with the Task Force of the Native American Comprehensive Plan (NACP). NACP is one of the national racial-ethnic plans authorized and funded by General Conference in order to reach out to particular communities. It was noted that no small group curriculum resource focusing on Native Americans had been produced within The United Methodist Church in over ten years. The decision was made to invite a variety of Native American United Methodist contributors on a variety of topics important to Native Americans.

The decision was also made to invite an eminent Native American ceremonial person to contribute articles to the book. By the term "ceremonial person" it is meant someone who lives their life within their tribal community and participates in the traditional tribal rituals of worship. There was a very short list of names. At the top of the list was Henrietta Mann, a Cheyenne woman who was, additionally, a well-respected scholar.

A second person invited to write for this publication was the Executive Director of NACP, Rev. Anita Phillips. Anita had written for a variety of Native and non-Native publications and had the experience of traveling extensively to meet with and visit Native Americans across the country. Additionally, prior to entering the ministry, she worked as a clinical social worker with Native American children and families for over twenty years. It is Anita's voice that serves as guide and navigator, weaving around and between the many voices of this book.

Anita made the initial journey to meet with Henri, as she came to be known, and presented the concept for the book. Fortunately,

Henri's response was positive, but with some reservations. To many Native Americans the Christian Church has not been a trustworthy institution, as readers of this book will learn. However, the partnership proved to be fruitful, growing into a friendship built upon mutual respect and appreciation.

The ten Native Americans invited to write on a variety of topics are both clergy and lay persons. Chosen for their life experiences and professional expertise, they have not merely written as observers, but have shared of the richness of their spiritual journeys. Each essay is offered as a gift to the reader, testifying to the amazing diversity of experience within the Native American community.

Also included is the voice of an indigenous person beyond the boundaries of the United States. Rev. Liberato Bautista, whose homeland is the Philippines, offers a powerful witness of his own path and that of his country. His ministry at the United Nations on behalf of the General Board of Church and Society and the entire church, has provided a depth of experience, resulting in great wisdom to be shared.

The combination of voices within *On This Spirit Walk* make for a dynamic mix of conversations. The contrast and comparison of essays allow the reader to trace common threads and discern differences.

Finally, each chapter concludes with a set of questions designed to help the small group process their responses to what was read. The questions are written to enable non-Native persons, as well as Native Americans and indigenous persons, to participate in the follow-up discussion session.

On This Spirit Walk offers to its readers the opportunity to hear voices typically drowned out by the dominant culture. There is wisdom and truth here. There is joy in the little things and respect for the forces of nature. There is hope offered by those who are least likely to be hopeful and understanding offered by those least understood. The authors offer themselves as instruments aimed at building a better life for all. May all who read be blessed.

Chapter 1

Identity

Human identity is an essential part of the wholeness of humanity. We might consider it an overarching principle that has its origins in the makeup of a person from birth, combined with and informed by the life experiences of that individual and by the groups to which the individual belongs. As we grow from infant to child, from child into youth and then into adulthood, our identity continues to develop.

For Christians, identity as followers of Jesus Christ is a primary part of who we are. We strive to live out our lives as disciples according to this identity. As we pass through the many stages of life, our Christian faith informs and shapes our decisions, career, relationships, and all the other components that make up our identity.

For Native Americans, identity as tribal peoples born of a particular nation, clan, band or tribal town is also a primary part of who we are. Native Americans live out of the identity of being indigenous peoples to various degrees according to a variety of factors. For some Native Americans, factors such as living far from tribal lands and reservations, being adopted by non-Indian parents, or intermarriage with other racial-ethnic groups leads to minimizing the impact of Native identity. However, for a great number of Native Americans in this nation, walking our path each day involves claiming all that Creator God has poured into us as indigenous peoples. We think and act in ways that are substantively different from our brothers and sisters from other racial-ethnic groups. Sociologists and educators have studied people whose identity grows out of being Native American. We do indeed experience differently such vital concepts as spirituality, time, space, family and relationships.

I came to know Dr. Henrietta Mann in the context of co-editing and writing for this book. As I have come to know and appreciate the person she is, I have realized how fully her identity is Native American, and more specifically, her identity is Cheyenne. In the following article she shares from her perspective on the topic of identity.

Each person possesses a unique personal identity made up of certain qualities or characteristics and holds an understanding of self as a distinct human being. Personal identity is basic, and there are other types which include gender, culture, ethnicity, spiritual/religious, or group identity. Ultimately identity is complex, but suffice it to say that Native Americans nurture identity as early as the period of gestation.

The expectant mother is encouraged to be the personification of peace and a model of calmness and patience, lest she become agitated or excited and affect the development of the life she is carrying. Oftentimes, the baby is spoken to or serenaded with song. The pregnant woman also must refrain from eating certain foods, which might impair normal development, mar physical appearance, or cause a difficult birth.

Welcoming

Cheyennes have a welcoming ceremony in which an elder introduces the infant to the spirits of the four directions and offers a prayer for the health and longevity of this new human being. Then the baby is passed around the circle to all those present. They each lovingly cuddle the baby and talk to it, expressing wishes for a good life, essentially welcoming the baby who has joined them on the road of life which they collectively walk as a people. It is important to note that the child's personal identity is established within the

family and with the cultural and group identity of the people.
A family member makes a decorated buckskin pouch, the shape of which is determined by gender, which could be either an elongated diamond, lizard, or turtle. The dried umbilical cord is encased in the pouch and is attached to a cradle, worn on a belt as a female child matures, and is carried for life. This object, it is believed, helps to stabilize the individual's behavior, personality, or personal identity.

Naming

Then there are native names. They are customarily given early in life and are usually bestowed ceremonially. A name can even be changed when one has achieved high honors or has shown great courage or bravery. Names are important because they serve to guide a person's life. For example, the name "Prayer Woman" forever mandates that individual's actions and how she is to be. She must live accordingly, and assume responsibilities for the spiritual health of the people, and minister to them when called upon. A family usually has a reservoir of names that have been passed down through the generations and have stayed within the family. They act as identifiers and also are a way of keeping the memory of a person alive.

Names took on another dimension in reservation schools and off-reservation boarding schools, the most infamous of which is Carlisle Indian Industrial Training School located in Pennsylvania. Children who attended such schools were forced to take Anglo names or Anglicized versions of their names. One female student whose father's name was Horse Road was given the surname Rhoades. To these children such names were entirely devoid of meaning.

Commencing in 1568 with the establishment of Jesuit schools for Florida native children, the Church has dominated the first three hundred years of the education of Native Americans. Such schools were intent upon assimilation in which everything native was to be eradicated and replaced with Christianity, civilization, and education. Native languages bore the frontal assault of assimilation in English-only schools. The very identity of these children was threatened personally, culturally, and spiritually. They were subjected harshly to a methodical break up of everything they were in terms of their ethnic identity, the effects of which can still be felt in the twenty-first century.

— Dr. Henrietta Mann

Historical Trauma

Because of the tragic, destructive, and genocidal history of Native Americans in the U.S. a unique ailment affecting mind, body and spirit has been identified as impacting many Native Americans today. It is called *historical trauma* and it is derived from massive suffering visited upon a people across life spans and generations. Over time, the suffering and wounding accumulates within the people both individually and collectively and their unresolved grief becomes overwhelming. Experiencing near extinction through loss of homeland, military imprisonment, exposure to infectious disease, loss of children to boarding schools and many other causes, tribal peoples in this country have borne the brunt of great cultural, social and physical oppression. For far too many Native Americans today, this grief is lived out as depression, alcohol and drug abuse, personal and family disintegration and domestic violence.

Boe Harris is a gifted Native flute player and poet who serves as the co-chair of her annual conference's Committee on Native American Ministries. She is also a gold medalist for softball in the U.S. Senior Olympics. This Turtle Mountain Chippewa/Spirit Lake Dakota woman for all seasons shares with us about the formation of her multifaceted identity.

Who Am I? Why Am I Here?

From the dawn of time humanity has asked the universal questions,"Who Am I?" and "Why Am I Here?" For some, these answers come early in life, but for me, I have had to grow into the questions and become and *live out* the answers.

So God created humankind in his image,
in the image of God he created them;
male and female he created them.
(Genesis 1:27)

On January 12, 1946, Creator God's breath of pure Spirit was breathed into my human form and my earth journey began.

I walk my earth journey as a descendant of native tribes from my mother's people and my father's people. My young life up until the age of 18 years was spent as a dependent of a father serving in the military. This lifestyle did not place us in any one location for any length of time and never near or on our home reservations or around our tribal people. In my younger years I knew little of who I was as a Native person and this left me feeling different, detached, and void of identity. As my father shared more about our tribal people and our culture, deeply rooted in traditions, values, customs, relationships with the earth, the Creator, Spirit and all living things, the answer to "Who Am I?" became clearer and gave me such comfort and a stronger sense of self.

Those Who Walked Before Me

I began to learn more about many of those ancestors who have walked before me. I felt knowing about where I came from gave me insight and a sense of the direction I might need to go. On this quest I asked myself the question, "Are there journeys I need to continue to take into the future, carrying on from those who have walked in the past?" Little did I know, early on in my quest, that the answers would be the foundation for my present day walk.

I didn't need to go far back into my family tree to discover an interesting, yet confusing, relationship with Christianity. My father was put into Indian boarding school at the age of five on his home reservation. This school was operated by a Christian church and it seemed their goal was to take the Indian out of the children, so they could become good, white Christian boys and girls.

7

As I was growing up my father insisted I go to church and to youth classes to learn more about the church, God and Jesus. Learning about God and this man, Jesus, interested me. However, when I got into my teen years I was questioning why I was going to a church that tried to take my father's identity away and create in him a new one.

When questioning my father about what happened in boarding school and why the church wanted to change him into someone he wasn't, few answers were given. It took me years to understand that my father only knew what he experienced and those experiences left him with suppressed pain and unresolved trauma. They also left him with few parenting skills The skills he did have echoed his boarding school experience of food to eat, roof over your head, discipline, skills to survive, unquestioned devotion to church and not knowing how to emotionally relate and express love from father to daughter. I also learned there were some questions he just couldn't answer. So I ventured upon my own quest to understand the relationship between the Church and Native people.

The Spirit in Me

This quest to better understanding has taken me on many paths, and led me to many discoveries. One discovery was an awareness of my self in relationship to my own spirituality. I have had a strong sense of Spirit since I was young. I can't recall when I first recognized this relationship between me and Spirit. It seems it has always been there, in me and with me, strong, powerful, protective, comforting and empowering. When I was young I did not have a name for this feeling of relationship to Spirit. I related to it as an imaginary friend, a non visible entity that was always with me.

I believe so strongly that we are born of pure Spirit, a gift and a blessing from the Holy of Holies. When we recognize that this Spirit lives within all living things, we deepen our relationship with the Creator and with others walking this life journey with us. Spirit is the essence of my cultural traditions and my Christian traditions. It is a medium through which individuals establish communication with the Holy. We all need this relationship with Spirit. It is our first and most powerful source of strength when life's path has many challenges. I have learned that I must stay close to Spirit. It is the foundation and source for maintaining my balance and an integral part of my identity.

As I continued my quest of understanding the relationship between the Church and Native people, I followed many paths. One path was that of anger at the Church, any church. They could not answer the question of why they wanted to change a person's cultural identity. They could not even admit that this process was wrong and left people scarred and damaged. So I spent many years avoiding Christianity and the Church.

On one path I spent time searching for the common thread among many world religions. This journey I found to be most interesting and enlightening. In one of these world religions I was surprised that Jesus was regarded with great respect and honor. Hearing this was a pivotal point in my journey. It opened me up to take another look at Christianity and this man, Jesus.

Jesus, a Tribal Man

In the pages of the Old Testament I am reminded that Jesus comes from a tribe, with the cultural traditions of language, clothing, songs, dance, festivals and prayers. While Jesus was upon this earth he worshiped and celebrated his father, God, with the traditions of his people.

Jesus, a man created in the image of God, God's own son, traveled the earth with cultural and spiritual identity to share the news of his father above.

So God created humankind in his image,
in the image of God he created them;
male and female he created them.
(Genesis 1:27)

When thinking about identity, I find that it is multifaceted. I have a spiritual identity, cultural identity, physical identity, an identity formed from life experiences and choices made, and the identity of being created in the image of God. It has taken most of my life's journey to understand how each facet of my identity is interrelated, and how each facet can come into balance and move me, with confidence, onto the path that I recognize I have been called to walk.

This path has taken me back into the Christian Church and to the question I once asked myself, "Are there journeys I need to continue to take into the future carrying on from those who have walked in the past?" I could not have answered this question until I grew into knowing who I am. Yes, I do need to take into the future the journeys of those who have walked in the past.

Why Am I Here? I am here to bring better understanding of the relationship between the Church and Native people, so that the walk of future generations is made with respect, celebrating who they are, created by God in his own image.

Boe Harris/Nakakakena
Turtle Mountain Chippewa/Spirit Lake Dakota
St. John's United Methodist Church
Co-chair, Conference Committee on Native American Ministry
Peninsula-Delaware Conference

Questions for Discussion

1. Dr. Mann shared from her culture about traditions of welcoming and naming. What important traditions exist in your tribe, nation, church or family? How do these traditions contribute to your identity?
2. Do you see the church today as contributing to the continuing negative impact of historical trauma in the lives of Native Americans or as contributing to the healing?
3. As you consider how your own identity was formed, what part did "those who walked before" play in shaping who you are?
4. What were the milestones that shaped your spiritual identity?

Chapter 2

Values

Every day we walk upon this earth, we carry our values along with us. These values both shape us and simultaneously are shaped by us. We find that we hold unique, individual values which we experience as individual persons, and we also hold shared, group values which we experience as part of larger population(s) to which we belong.

Native American people belong to one or more native tribes or nations. Each tribe is a distinct cultural entity with its own values, customs and language. However, there are broad categories of values to which most tribes relate. As I have travelled to different parts of the U.S. I have found this to be true. One example of a shared value which I have happily come across in my travels is the shared value of humor. There is a unique take on all of the troubles and barriers we face in our lives—and it is reflected in our humor. While we understand the seriousness of our circumstances, we share the belief that laughing at our hardships helps us survive them. We do truly believe that laughter is good medicine, but a downcast spirit dries up the bones (Proverbs 17:22). Humor can offer a good entry into a different Native community. I have been in a new setting with people from different tribes, and after sharing a few laughs, doors will open on new relationships.

Dr. Henrietta Mann and I are from two very different tribes from distinct parts of the country, each with unique histories. Yet, as we got to know one another, we found that we shared a great deal and had many common values. In the following essay, she discusses values and the actions that correlate with them.

Giving As a Way of Life

Native Americans are traditionally a giving and sharing people, and they are noted for their generosity. Their world views are based upon the concept of interdependence in which they recognize their dependence upon everything else in life. Reciprocity is the rule, and there is a fundamental give and take. They continue to acknowledge the generosity of Mother Earth, who since creation has held them lovingly in her lap and supports their feet. In return Native people renew her through their ceremonies. Earth also nourishes them by providing necessary sustenance, such as food directly by vegetation and indirectly by game birds, deer, bison, and cattle. In addition, the trees and plants rooted in her soil provide human beings with vital oxygen and human beings reciprocate by providing them with carbon dioxide.

Giveaways – Living in Thankfulness

Native Americans know the Earth as their first and spiritual mother, who models generosity for them. They have institutionalized this generosity into giveaways which are ceremonial acts of sharing with the community. The tradition of giveaways is known by different names and observed differently by different tribal groups. Northwest coast people hold elaborate potlatch ceremonies. The Pueblos of the southwest observe their feast days and throw gifts from the tops of their homes. Plains people, those of the Midwest, and others have giveaways.

A unique aspect of giveaways is that a person being honored is the one who gives gifts or a relative gives in his/her behalf, rather than being given gifts. Sometimes, the measure of love for the person so honored determines the amount of material goods given. In a special Cheyenne ceremony, the love for a person is gauged by how high off the ground a person sits on a stack of giveaway items.

Family members may have a giveaway at some public event to observe a birthday, the first time a child dances, receiving a name, welcoming a soldier home, or other such momentous occasions. There is a wonderful story about a young soldier returning from Iraq who walked on a path of Pendleton blankets laid end to end from the time he exited the plane at the gate, all the way through the airport, to the family automobile parked at the curb outside. All the Pendletons were given away, which demonstrates how Native peoples honor their veterans. Based on this story, one can understand the statement of a parent who stated "I am a poor man because I love my children so much." Native people love to give and a pow wow would not be a pow wow without giveaways, which are a time-honored tradition of sharing.

The Poor Become Rich Through Giving

Giveaways do not always involve sharing high-priced material items, nor are they all public. Some are very private. A simple Native custom is to always give something to a visitor to one's home, even if it is nothing more than a drink of water. Should one go to seek knowledge or cultural information, it is usual for that person to take a gift to the person who is the keeper of the information in return for the sharing of treasured ancient knowledge or wisdom. A wise Native elder, who had accumulated little wealth in his life time, told his son as he was nearing death, "I have nothing to leave you but my words." What a precious gift and a giveaway of the heart and spirit.

Native hunters usually give thanks to an animal for giving its life to feed the people. Those who pick plant people, such as sage or sweet grass, must make an offering of some type, such as tobacco. People make tobacco offerings as they send out their prayers to the powers of the four directions, to the earth, and to the Great All Giving Spirit of the universe. Reciprocity and mutuality are living Native traditions.

Dr. Henrietta Mann

One afternoon, over a year ago, we met at Dr. Mann's office in Weatherford, Oklahoma where she serves as President of the

Cheyenne and Arapaho Tribal College. After working for a few hours, we prepared to end our meeting. She shared that later that day she would be helping a student to prepare for her giveaway at a pow wow later in the week. Like most students, I'm sure this young woman had very limited resources. Dr. Mann was preparing to search through her own closets for items she could share with this student—in essence a giveaway that would lead to another giveaway!

Carol Lakota Eastin is an ordained elder in the Illinois Great Rivers Conference. She was the founding pastor for the most recent Native American church to be chartered in the North Central Jurisdiction, Dayspring United Methodist Church in East Peoria, Illinois. Carol will represent her annual conference later this year as a 2012 jurisdictional delegate. In her buckskin dress, she has proudly danced with her Native American brothers and sisters at powwows; and from her pulpit she has proudly and humbly preached to Native and non-Native alike. In the essay that follows, she shares of her life and the values that shaped the person she is.

I Love a People – American Indian Values

I grew up in the projects on the south side of Peoria, Illinois, one of three daughters of two mixed blood parents. Our heritage includes Lakota, Yakama, Shawnee, French and Irish. In our neighborhood people knew we were Native American, not so much because they recognized our last name, "Lakota," as an Indian name, but because we were the family that had a teepee in our yard in the summer and went to the local park to shoot the bows and arrows my dad made by hand. We didn't speak our indigenous language. We grew up in the city. And that pretty much made us typical urban American Indians of the latter half of the twentieth century.

An Indian World View

As our people moved into cities, spoke English, adopted European American customs, attended school and church, there was something that always made us "different." I remember thinking as a child that we were from a different planet. It turns out that we were at home in America; it was just that a lot of people around us were from another world. What seems to have remained in the minds and hearts of my parents, and which was passed on to us girls, was an Indian worldview...a way of seeing things...and a way of being.

So, some things were different for us. My dad never believed in going into debt, so we rented an apartment, and never owned a car. We walked or rode the bus. Owning things wasn't important to him. I remember he had this tattered winter coat and my mother kept asking him to buy a new one. Finally, he gave in and bought a new winter coat at Montgomery Wards. It was hanging in the closet next to his old one, when a knock came on the door. It was one of the homeless guys from downtown. "Hey Johnny," he said to my dad, "It's getting cold out here. Do you have an old coat I could have?" Perfect, we thought, Dad will finally get rid of that old tattered coat. He walked over to the closet and took out the new coat, tags still hanging from it, and gave it to the visitor. After he closed the door, we asked, "Why did you do THAT?" And he answered simply, "He needs it more than I do."

A Contrast of Values

Below is a list of contrasts that demonstrate why many American Indians find it difficult to achieve a balance between their values and the values of the dominant society.

American Indian Values	Majority Culture American Values
Value the person	Value a person's possessions
Great respect for elders	Idealizing youthfulness
Sharing of material goods	Private ownership
Humility	Competitiveness
Honoring past traditions	Future orientation/ planning
Emphasize the mystical	Emphasize the scientific
Harmony with nature	Dominating nature
Community cooperation	Individualism/ Independence

Recently, I was leading a retreat for a group of United Methodist clergy, and one of them asked me if I could talk about how I reconcile my American Indian beliefs and values with being a Christian. I smiled and remarked that I would like to hear him talk about how he reconciles being a twenty-first-century citizen of the United States with being a Christian. In actuality, many of the values held by Native people fit closely with the values of the early Christian community.

Now the whole group of those who believed were of one heart and soul, and no one claimed private ownership of any possessions, but everything they owned was held in common. (Acts 4:32)

Believers were part of an extended family, and connection to that family rather than individualism was valued.

I am the vine, you are the branches. Those who abide in me and I in them bear much fruit, because apart from me you can do nothing. (John 15:5)

Jesus and his disciples modeled a simple and selfless lifestyle. Jesus stressed that spiritual freedom comes from emptying oneself.

Then he said to them all, "If any want to become my followers, let them deny themselves and take up their cross daily and follow me. For those who want to save their life will lose it, and those who lose their life for my sake will save it. What does it profit them if they gain the whole world, but lose or forfeit themselves? (Luke 9:23-25)

Catlin's Creed

George Catlin is a well-known artist who spent eight years living among Indians of the Great Plains. In 1868 he wrote, "I have visited 48 different tribes, and feel authorized to say that the North American Indian in his native state is honest, hospitable, faithful, brave, and an honorable and religious human being." The following excerpt is sometimes called "Catlin's Creed."

*I love a people that have always made me welcome to
the very best that they had.
I love a people who are honest without laws, who have
no jails and no poorhouses.
I love a people who keep the commandments without ever
having read or heard them preached from the pulpit.
I love a people who never swear or take the name of
God in vain.
I love a people "who love their neighbors as they love
themselves."
I love a people who worship God without a Bible, for I
believe that God loves them also.
I love a people whose religion is all the same, and who
are free from religious animosities.
I love a people who have never raised a hand against
me, or stolen my property, when there was no law to
punish either.
I love and don't fear mankind where God has made
and left them, for they are his children.
I love the people who have never fought a battle with
the white man, except on their own ground.
I love a people who live and keep what is their own
without lock and keys.
I love a people who do the best they can. And oh how I
love a people who don't live for the love of money.[1]*

As a Native American Christian, I am very comfortable in my
skin. I really can't say I've experienced much conflict between the
values of my people and my relationship with Jesus. However, my
knowledge of the history of Christianity, the church's relationship with
indigenous persons, and my own experience of it, is another story.

Carol Lakota Eastin
Lakota/Yakama
Elder
Illinois Great Rivers Conference

Questions for Discussion

1. How do you reconcile your values with being a child of God?
2. Name one or two values of great importance to your life. How do these values relate to the values Jesus taught?
3. Is there congruence between your talk and your walk?
4. Are your personal values a closer reflection of American Indian Values or Majority Culture American Values or a mix of both? Share examples from your experience.

1. Catlin George. Episodes from "Life Among the Indians" and "Last Rambles". Mineola, NY: Dover Publications, Inc.; 1997: 354-355. (Used by permission)

Chapter 3

Relationship

The first two chapters of the Book of Genesis have the power to teach us a great deal about relationship. When God, the Solitary, became God, the Creator, relationship was born, along with all of Creation. One of the greatest gifts humanity has ever received is the chance to live and breathe in the medium of relationship.

As I have worked alongside Dr. Mann for nearly a year and a half, a subtext to the work of this book developed in the form of our relationship. I come from the Keetoowah Cherokee people who originated in the southeastern U.S. My people were historically hunters and farmers who lived in villages. We were one of many tribes forced onto death marches which came to be called "Trails of Tears." Henri (as Dr. Henrietta Mann invited me to call her), came from a people who were migratory across the northern and central plains. She is a Cheyenne enrolled with the Cheyenne and Arapaho Tribes located in Oklahoma. Her people followed the buffalo and moved according to the seasons until the U.S. Government forced them into military stockades and ultimately, to reservations. As she shared stories from her life and her people, I did the same, and we came to know each other at a deeper level.

In the following essay, Henri eloquently describes the nature of relationships from an indigenous perspective.

We Are All Related

Relationship is about relatedness; it is kinship; it is connection; it is about interdependence and reciprocity. The Native peoples of this land accept the fact that they exist in a colossal universe in which everything is kin, and that they live in a mammoth ocean of relations. Long ago their remarkable scientists and philosophers studied life and determined that everything is made up of the same four elements. These elements are water, earth, air, and sunlight or fire.

The Four Elements of Relationship

Life begins in water and for nine months human life is nourished, protected, cherished, and blessed by the waters of the mother's womb. The human body is as much as 75 percent water making it related to that which falls from the sky, flows in rivers and streams, stands in oceans and ponds, and is stored in underground aquifers. It is also related to its different forms of ice, mist, vapor, or steam. Since all life forms, too, are water, then everything is kin and are family.

The kinship connection to earth makes humans related to the dust, soil, clay, and mud from which they are made. Human beings also are related to rocks, the oldest part of earth. It makes them related to the volcanoes, mountains, buttes, and valleys, essentially every geographic aspect of the land which supports and carries life. This land or earth is a spirit mother and native people have an umbilical-like connection to her. They are attached to land, which they love as one would love a mother, and they hold this land or earth in great reverence.

Then there is the third element, air. Air is that invisible, colorless, odorless, and untouchable element that surrounds, protects, and cushions all life. It is the breath of Mother Earth. According to some native origin accounts, after the humble upright two-legged walkers were made, Creator called the winds from their homes in the four directions to come give them the breath of life. Again, since everything is made of air, all life is related. This kindred connection includes the winds, gentle breezes, tiny whirlwinds, tornadoes, and violent hurricanes.

Fire or sunlight is the fourth element from which all life is made. Creator brought light into existence to illuminate the darkness and to warm the earth and all life. Human beings have a fire hidden within that maintains a normal temperature of 98.6 degrees. The spark of life can be seen in the sparkle of the eyes and felt in the warmness of the hands. The intense heat can be felt in a purifying, cleansing, healing, and renewing sweat lodge ceremony. Because all life is made up of fire, then the lava flowing out of active volcanoes and that gigantic orb that rises on the eastern horizon each morning, too, are relatives.

A Cosmic Understanding of Relationship

Because everything is a relative to each other and life exists in a relational universe, an individual must think inclusively about life. Kinship is not limited to one's family, but it incorporates everything that exists as one universal family, the range of diversity that comprises the sum total of humanity, and by extension it incorporates everything that crawls, walks on two-legs or four, flies, or stands rooted in the ground. Expanding ever outward, it includes the sun, moon, stars, planets, and everything that exists in the far reaches of intergalactic space. All life exists within the one great circle of life, described by Black Elk as the sacred hoop of the world.

It practically defies the ability of the human imagination to visualize the magnitude of the cosmos that is incorporated in the circle of life. In that circle, everything and everyone is equal and stands in proper relationship as a good relative each to one another, as well as with the sun, moon, stars, oceans, rivers, mountains, the four winds, and all human beings regardless of who they are and where they live.

American Indian philosophers acknowledge that life exists in a relational universe that is teeming with life. All life is connected and everything is kin, and what happens to one happens to all. This relational universe is characterized by interdependence in which all life depends on other life forms for existence. Interdependence is dependent upon respect, mutuality, reciprocity, and accepting one's responsibility for all life. At a basic level it translates into everyone being responsible for the small place each occupies in the vast circle of life. Thus, the two-legged walkers must realize that they have a primary responsibility for treating their only home Planet Earth with sincere love and utmost respect. That is what makes a good relative.

Dr. Henrietta Mann

Phyllis Singing Bird is a woman of great gifts and deep commitment. Through her grandparents, she learned the art of healing with plants and herbs. Phyllis is the author of two books: a Native American Sunday School Curriculum and a book on using herbs in a practical way. Phyllis is also a certified lay speaker, mother, grandmother, fighter of racism, and devoted servant of the Creator. Here, she shares with us bits and pieces of her life and the importance of relationships along the way.

On This Journey Together

I therefore, the prisoner in the Lord, beg you to lead a life worthy of the calling to which you have been called, with all humility and gentleness, with patience, bearing with one another in love, making every effort to maintain the unity of the Spirit in the bond of peace. There is one body and one Spirit, just as you were called to the one hope of your calling, one Lord, one faith, one baptism, one God and Father of all, who is above all and through all and in all.
(Ephesians 4:1-6)

Allow me to translate this scripture in the way my grandmother would have said it, "Our Sacred Father is in everything, made everything, controls everything and loves everything."

I learned about relationships through the teachers in my life. I want to share with you the history of my teachers. To do that I will take you back to my childhood, sitting around the dining room table on Sundays or on a holiday with my family. I see my grandmother.

She is seated at one end of the table. Grandmother was of the Mohawk Nation and she was a medicine teacher. At the other end of the table sits my grandfather. He was of the Seneca Nation and a keeper of the stories. I can see my uncle who was a United Methodist minister. Across from him sits my mother. Mom was a medical missionary for The United Methodist Church. My father was a professional boxer and a dedicated horse trainer, and along with my two sisters, is also there at the table. My sister Pat was seven years older than me, and Penny was two years younger. Penny is a special person. She is a "little person" and was born with physical and mental challenges.

Learning Through Relationships

My mother, I am proud to say, was my best friend and my closest teacher. I want to share with you about her "bad" habit that drove us girls crazy. Mom loved to give. Momma said that when you could sacrifice and give from the heart, it was just like giving to God. Believe me when I say this, God got a lot of our stuff! Mom would sing an old-time Gospel hymn and then we would sit down to eat at the table. Often we were joined by several "poor, needy souls" Mom had brought home from church. We would ask for blessings and express our gratitude for our meal along with the several guests. We hardly got a taste of the awesome stew that had been simmering while we were at church. Our meal ended up heavy on the crackers and milk.

I learned about the power of relationship with "the least of these" from my mother. When we would least expect it, there would be a knock at the door and the "poor, needy souls" would be standing there with tears in their eyes saying thank you, and giving back all they had gotten and usually more!

My mother and my uncle told me they learned about faith and the Sacred Father from their mother, my grandmother, the medicine teacher who had never stepped into a church ever.

One of my earliest memories is being stung by a bumblebee. I was on a medicine walk with my grandmother. She said some prayers, put some tobacco down and thanked the plantain for its

25

medicine to heal me. She picked a leaf, mashed it up and rubbed its juices on the bite. The pain was instantly gone. By the time we arrived home you almost couldn't find where I had been stung.

Life with grandmother was a busy life and a blessed life, too. There were many traditional stories that taught life lessons. They were filled with respect for the plant and animal brothers and sisters as well as for all humans. The Creator breathed his breath of life into us all. That makes us all equal and necessary to each other to live and survive. We must live in relationship with one another.

No longer does the word "medicine" only mean the prescription that we buy. Sometimes it means what the plant or animal brothers and sisters teach us. By watching them, we humans can learn of their strengths and weaknesses. We even rely on them for nourishment. The smell that fills us with joy, the beauty that makes our hearts sing, food that fills our tummies or just the pure wonder of nature, both the plants and animals are good medicine.

Sacred Rules to Live By

My mother, grandmother and grandfather taught me that there are three important rules to live by.

First, you must say thank you to our Creator before you receive. Before you harvest food or medicine, you say thank you. Before you go on the hunting trip, you say thank you. Before the person who is sick becomes well (physically or spiritually), we say thank you. Not only do we say thank you, but we give a gift to show our Creator that we know our prayers will be answered.

Second, and this is a step that is hard to do, we must accept any burden or challenge we may face and see it as an opportunity or lesson from which to learn. We may not like what has happened and, at the time, we usually do not understand what we can learn from the lesson. I am talking about the hard things of life such as the death of a loved one or, like my little sister, a person with physical or mental challenges.

The third and final step brings blessing and healing to us. This happens when we reach out to help others through what we have learned. It is our obligation to use what we learn in life to help someone else.

Let me tell you about Christopher James. He was a beautiful baby boy born to a young couple in December of 1972. He was our second son. Our first son, Billy, was 2 years old. Our family was happy and every day seemed to be blessed. Then in March there came a reason to celebrate. Christopher had slept through the night for the first time.

But when I slid my hand under him to pick him up, he was ice cold! This cold thing was not my baby—I questioned God! Why me? What had I ever done to deserve this? What had my baby done? I questioned my faith and I knew there was not any good that could come from this horror.

Relationship Comes Full Circle

Two years later, I sat in the emergency room in Baumholder, Germany with a horrible migraine headache. As I sat there waiting to be seen, a woman came running out of the treatment room screaming, "My baby is not dead!" With my headache forgotten, I followed her. I did not want to go, but I think God put a magnet in me because I had no choice. I did my best to comfort her. Finally she yelled at me as she beat on my chest with her fists "How can you tell me everything will be O.K.?" I knew because I had been through it too! Dianne and I started a support group for Sudden Infant Death Syndrome for folks in the military. It was so necessary being far from home and family.

Yes, there was good that could come from the death of my precious infant son. All that we go through in life offers us something to learn. Because we live in relationship with one another, we must use what we learn to help one another.

This thing called life is amazing. Our Sacred Father is in everything, made everything, controls everything and loves everything.

Phyllis Singing Bird
Seneca/Mohawk
Dayspring United Methodist Church
Illinois Great Rivers Conference

Questions for Discussion

1. Have you ever been surprised to form a positive relationship with someone very different from you? What part did your faith play in helping you to build a bridge to connect with this other person?
2. How do you respond to the idea that we are related to all of Creation through the four elements of water, earth, air and sunlight or fire? Share an example of how you feel related to parts of Creation that are not humans.
3. When you learn about Native American leaders such as Black Elk or Phyllis Singing Bird, who remain faithful to their traditional Native ways, and also adopt the Christian faith, how do you view these persons? What internal or external conflicts might arise when someone wants to include both in their life?
4. How does the scripture from Ephesians quoted at the beginning of Phyllis Singing Bird's essay speak to you about the nature of relationship as a Native American follower of Jesus Christ?

Chapter 4

Storytelling

I have been privileged in my life to know many storytellers. Some were from my own tribe and some from other tribes. I have tried to remember the techniques that most appealed to me and incorporate these into the stories I tell my grandchildren. On long trips in the car, I have had good opportunities to be an amateur storyteller. It seems that children are uniquely formed to grasp the meaning of stories and to respond with pure, unfettered emotion to the funny, scary, moving, exciting, and sad stories they hear. Perhaps this was one of the reasons Jesus pointed to children as an example for the rest of us.

Among the stories from my tribe, the Cherokee Nation, one of my favorites is the story of how the world came to have fire. It was Grandmother Spider who had the resourcefulness and courage to carry fire from the sun in a pottery basket. I celebrate that females and elders are an honored part of of the story of my people.

Henri, as I now call her, turned 77 years of age while we worked on this book together. She works long days to make the Cheyenne and Arapaho Tribal College a place where her people can become educated and take their place in the world. Tribal colleges may be found on many reservations and in Oklahoma, and are designed to enhance educational opportunities for the poorest Native Americans. Through Henri's calling in this life, I believe I have witnessed the same resourcefulness and courage as that of Grandmother Spider. As you read her essay, imagine you can hear her speaking to you. Listen to the storyteller.

Storytellers – Prophets for the People

Native Americans have always placed a great value upon words because they are created by air as it vibrates against the vocal folds. Air is the sacred breath of life and the breath of Earth. Native people have preserved their cultures through the language of words and through language express their relationship to all of life about them. Thus, they are a people of words and of oral traditions, which include prayer, conversation, oratory, song, and stories. Stories are of great magnitude because they encapsulate cultures; contain a people's origins, theology, and migrations; explain why the world is the way it is; are a people's history and literature; and preserve tribal values and environmental ethics that have sustained them on the road of life. Thus, storytelling plays a vital cultural role, and so do storytellers, who are respected and have the crucial responsibility of keeping essential traditional knowledge.

Storytellers had extraordinary memories and they were usually fluent language speakers. Parents often invited storytellers to their lodge where a feast was served and gifts provided for the privilege of once again hearing stories of times past. Certain protocol governed storytelling. Once the sharing began, the lodge door was secured and no one could enter, and all those inside were expected to be quiet and show respect. For some Native people their stories could be told only at night or only in the winter season, and there were consequences for recounting stories at unspecified times. Storytelling was a happy and exciting time and once children became aware that a storyteller had been invited or was coming to the encampment, they could hardly contain their anticipation. In a contemporary setting, it would be almost like visiting a library and listening to one audio book after another in complete astonishment.

No Limits to Native Stories

There are many kinds of Native American stories. There are sacred stories including those that deal with the genesis of a people, which fall into four categories. There are those whose beginnings are the result of a woman falling from the sky above or those who came to the earth from the stars. Another category recounts how some peoples came from successive worlds below and emerged to live on the surface of earth. Then there are those stories which tell how some water being brings up some mud from the bottom of the ocean which expands to become this island home of Native Americans. Finally there is a general category that includes stories that do not fall within any of the three groupings.

Also included in the sacred category are stories that deal with features of the landscape, such as mountain, butte, river, or waterfalls, which figure prominently in the life of the people. They recount important events that happened at those specific places, which mandate certain actions or ceremonies that must take place there regularly. Such places are classified as sacred sites, which must be protected for the roles they play in maintaining the earth and cultural continuity.

In addition there are stories of culture heroes, sometimes called prophets, who are sent from the Great Mysterious to bring a good message or ways that bring about positive and changed ways to the people. There are wondrous stories that explain how the constellations came into existence in the night sky; how some nations received the sweat lodge, other sacred ceremonies, or ceremonial objects; why animals and birds are the color they are and how they got their markings; why certain customs are adhered to; or how a person got a song. There also are stories of a more contemporary nature that tell of conflict and bravery, or an occurrence of monumental importance.

There are no limits to native stories, since they are about life. Not all of them are serious because native peoples place much emphasis upon humor. Some characters, who possess both creative and destructive attributes, who are called tricksters, walk in and out of native stories. They are often deceitful, dishonest, untrustworthy and teach through negative example. The Kiowa have Saynday; others have hare, rabbit, coyote, raven, or spider, to cite the more common ones. The Cheyenne have Vi-ho-I, a wanderer, who has the ability to concoct a logical explanation for any bizarre situation of his making; who wants knowledge but upon receiving it, handles it irresponsibly, and gets himself into trouble; and he appears to lack common sense.

Real Life is Also the Stuff of Stories

Stories inform, teach, extend back in time to the beginning, and are constantly adding to their repertoire. There are stories of new events or places, or of their heroes, such as Jim Thorpe, the Tall Chief ballerinas, Wilma Mankiller, and Will Rogers, to cite but a few. Storytellers continue to play a vital role in keeping native stories alive. Stories are still in the making as the younger generations, too, walk the Road of Life, which is a good road, a happy one, and which extends far into an unknown future. The storytellers of tomorrow will tell the stories of yesterday and today, and remember "when [in 1830] the stars fell," and they also will remember when in 2002 John B. Herrington, Chickasaw astronaut, became the first federally enrolled American Indian man to fly in space. They will remember how he traveled to the international space station on the Endeavour, walked in space three times, and looked down on earth from about 250 miles away. He visited the stars and walked among them. What a glorious story!

Dr. Henrietta Mann

One of the pleasures of serving The United Methodist Church in my present appointment is the opportunity to cross paths with so many gifted people. Raggatha Rain Calentine is one of these people. She is an extraordinary storyteller. When you see Ragghi rub her hands together and kick off her shoes, you know she is preparing to deliver a message from the Creator through her stories. The story and the storyteller become one, and we who listen are invited into the world of the story.

Ragghi is Co-Chair of her conference Committee on Native American Ministries, is a certified lay speaker, youth leader and advocate. In the essay that follows, she shares with us her witness of what it means to be a storyteller.

Chosen by the Giver of Breath

We do not choose to be storytellers. We are chosen to be the Keepers of Living Stories. With our breath, we give life to the stories and they take flight. Stories are powerful medicine. They can bring tears or laughter. Stories are often used to begin to heal hearts, to discipline, teach lessons, remember our history and recall how things came to be. We stand on sacred ground when telling a story. Slipping our shoes off to be closer to Our Earth Mother, it reminds us to give honor to The One and Only, the Giver of Breath, the Maker of All Things, for the gift of stories and the privilege to be a Keeper of Living Stories.

The Stories Stand on Their Own

As a small child I was taught you never walk alone. The One and Only walks with us, as well as those who have walked before us and have crossed over, those who are walking with us in the present time, and the future generations who walk with us. I learned to be careful of the way I walked and spoke. This is a very heavy load to carry, especially for a small child. I loved listening to stories, even when I didn't understand the story. It came as a great surprise when my father said, "You will be a storyteller." Born with a speech impediment, there wasn't a day that went by that I didn't hear someone laughing at me or telling me to speak slower. So after a while, I stopped speaking. How could I be a Keeper of Living Stories? A miracle happened when a teacher believed I was just tongue tied and found a way to get the help I needed. There are many words I still cannot speak, but WOW, hear the stories and you would never know. It is not about me and never will be. The stories stand on their own.

How do we put into words how stories change lives—not just other people's lives but our own life? I have had the unique jobs of teaching in schools for pregnant teens, in youth and adult prisons, in high risks areas, and anywhere else I could teach on the edge of life. I won't say it was easy, because it was not, but the gift of stories opened doors to hearts. Every lesson began with a story concerning the issues we would focus upon that day. How do you teach about forgiveness when the room is filled with anger, hate, loneliness, heartbreak? The story opened the door as we talked about the people in the story and their pain. We talked about what these people could do and where they could go from here. Then we talked about their own stories and what path they planned to travel. I'm still amazed, walking into the classroom and hearing, "What story today?" and "How about telling that funny one again?"

I often thought the stories were for others but really, they were also for me. I learned how to truly forgive after telling a story countless times about a child not wanted by her mother, to finally realize the lesson was also for me. I forgave and began to heal. The blanket story is a wonderful story that teaches respect for elders. The lesson comes from a small child. My Father taught me to care for others before myself, just like in our Indian communities. There is no word for "I," only the word for "we," for we never walk alone.

Stories of Grief and Laughter

Writing about the crossing over of a child, our son, Gabriel Eyes of the Deer, and telling of a mother's grief, has helped me walk in a different way. The death of a child is incredibly painful and still is. Writing and then telling the story of Caterpillar Woman and Caterpillar Man and the death of their child is still so painful, but it began a healing way for me. The story opens up conversation with others who share in the crossing over of a child or someone dear to them. One quote from the story is engraved upon my heart, "Caterpillar Woman pulled her grief around her like a shawl, and her falling tears became the fringe upon her shawl of sorrow." The importance of tears should always be remembered.

There are not only sad stories but funny stories with good endings, teaching about laughter as good medicine. There is a story about Turtle. The lesson is for the young and not so young, "There is a time to open your mouth, but more importantly, a time to keep it closed."

Native people were given the gift of stories, the wisdom of caring for each story and the knowledge of ways to use stories. Our lives are filled with lessons from the spoken word handed down from one to another.

Jesus, the Greatest Storyteller

Jesus told the crowds all these things in parables; without a parable he told them nothing. This was to fulfill what had been spoken through the prophet: "I will open my mouth to speak in parables; I will proclaim what has been hidden from the foundation of the world."
(Matthew 13:34-35)

Jesus used stories to teach the people and his teachings through stories are still retold to this day. When I think about the parable of the sower of seeds, I think about how Jesus planted seeds into our hearts and lives. Those seeds were called parables and they have taken root in our lives.

Take a moment and remember the stories Jesus taught—the lost sheep, the lost coin, the lost son (prodigal son). These are only a few of the teachings of the greatest storyteller, Jesus. When so much of what we hear and learn is forgotten, a story is remembered. Jesus painted pictures with his words and they can be seen forever.

We are the Keepers of Living Stories, whether they are parables from the Bible, Native American traditional stories, family stories, or so many other types of stories. The lessons from stories take root and live inside us.

On the day our children were born we wrapped them tight in a blanket of stories. Our children have grown and so have the stories, for our children now have stories of their own to tell. My father was a Keeper of Living Stories. When he was close to crossing over, we stayed in his room and told story after story. Those who came to visit sat and listened, then told a story or two before leaving. Father crossed over hearing the old stories and was wrapped in a blanket of stories for his final journey.

Ragghi Rain
Cherokee
Indian Mission United Methodist Church
Co-chair, Conference Committee on Native American Ministry
Peninsula-Delaware Conference

Questions for Discussion

1. Who have been the storytellers in your life? Share a description of the way that one of these persons made their stories come to life.
2. Have you ever been a storyteller in your family, church or tribe? Share about your experience in telling a story.
3. In Ragghi's essay, Jesus is called the greatest storyteller. What was the power of telling stories (parables) to the people of his day?
4. Briefly share a story that made an impact in your life. Have you passed this story on to others? Why or why not?

Chapter 5

Creation

I once heard a Native American scholar share his opinion that Native Americans had their own equivalent of the Hebrew Bible (Old Testament) in the form of their oral tradition which includes stories of creation, rules for relationship (laws) and prophecies. These stories, like those in the Hebrew Bible, range from the beautiful to the tragic, and from the dramatic to the mundane.

Creation stories are a fascinating aspect of a people. For my nation, our creation stories tell of how the animals played a part in helping the Creator bring forth the world. As is true in many stories of creation, the small and insignificant play a major part in our stories. It is the lowly water beetle that has the stamina to dive deep into the waters of birth and bring up a tiny spot of mud which grows into the islands of land upon the water-covered earth.

As Henri and I shared stories, including those of creation, we celebrated that the Great Mystery who created the Cheyenne people had also created the Cherokee people. In her essay on creation, Henri tells us of the great host of creation stories among Native Americans.

Creation's Holy Ground

The first holy being known by many different tribal names which include Creator, Earth Maker, First Maker, All Spirit, or Great Mysterious brought a vast universe into existence, oftentimes, however, relying upon the assistance of other beings. The indigenous homeland was an island, completely surrounded by water. The powerful spirits and winds of the four directions lived somewhere far out in the unfathomable space. According to other first nations' views, some things already existed. Regardless of the differing views of their sacred beginnings, they accept the reality that this place was holy ground when time began and life was new and pure. For them creation, *manéstoo'o* is an ongoing process and even the lowly human beings play a role in its continuation. Furthermore, they are related to everything that exists in this world with which they must live in reverent interdependence.

Of Mothers and Daughters

Native Americans honor the earth, which gives them life. Earth as spiritual mother models the maternal role women have in bringing forth life and loving and protecting their children as they nurture their development, thus assuring the continuity of the people. Beyond that women in various tribal societies have brought wonderful gifts and truths to the people. Take for example corn, a staple of life. The Cherokee revere Selu, who gave them the gift of corn from her body, which has sustained them since. Another revered view of corn is that of Corn Mother of the Pueblos. The Pueblos live in the arid lands of the American Southwest, and are the world's expert dry land farmers. As they hoe and irrigate their cornfields they sing to the corn, which comes in six colors that represent the six directions. In reciprocity, the corn gives them pollen which the Pueblos use in prayer to communicate with the holy people.

In the northeast region of the country, one finds the Haudenausaunee (Iroquois). Among them the Clan Mothers own the fields in the same way they own the children. In their traditions they grow the three plants of corn, beans, and squash which they refer to as the Three Sisters, which are plants of a divine origin. Like sisters who can live in the same house, the three plants can grow from the same hill, and together they create a natural nitrogen cycle that is beneficial to the growth of corn. Eaten together the Three Sisters provide a balanced nutritious meal and the Haudenausaunee give thanksgiving each day for the three, known as the sustainers of life.

The Lakota/Nakota/Dakota (Sioux) say that many centuries ago, White Buffalo Calf Woman came to them and brought a sacred bundle that contained a pipe, the symbol of truth. Over a period of four days she gave them seven sacred ceremonies, which embody their wonderful life-sustaining teachings that also maintain the health of the earth. She also taught them how to pray, to worship, and to live an ethical life through these ceremonies, which include the vision quest and sun dance. This powerful female holy being left them with the promise that she would return. The White Buffalo Calf Pipe is reverently kept on the Cheyenne River Reservation in South Dakota by nineteenth generation keeper Arvol Looking Horse.

In traditional Native societies women have played and still play a vital role in continuing to create as the universal community walks into the present and future. Selu, Corn Mother, the Three Sisters, and White Buffalo Calf Woman exemplify the respectful connections among plants, animals, humans, earth, the cosmos, and the divine. They bridge time and the generations. They provide a relationship with future daughters who will bring forth families who, too, will carry on their traditions and the process of creation.

Dr. Henrietta Mann

Fred Shaw is a man who lives in the midst of his tribal history and he brings that history to life. A recently retired elder, he is a renowned storyteller of the Shawnee people. Fred has an extensive history working with the Cincinnati Zoo in the preservation of wildlife and working with public education in sharing his Shawnee traditions. His exhilarating essay on creation reflects the awe with which he approaches the web of life.

Creation as the Heart of God

The beauty, exhilaration, and complexity of the world first drew me to God. That has been true for many people. The wonder and vastness of Creation stirs the human spirit to burst forth in exclamations of praise and awe for the Creator. (Psalm 8) You know the personality of an artist by what the artist creates. A plant ultimately identifies its nature by the kind of seed or fruit it produces. The character of a land reveals itself in the interconnections of life that coexist upon it. Paul believed that is true of God as well,

Ever since the creation of the world God's eternal power and divine nature, invisible though they are, have been understood and seen through the things God has made.
(Romans 1:20)

God as Creator

When the Creation's awesome reality overwhelms a person, questions of "Who?" and "Why?" naturally arise. The church now called United Methodist gave me the three biblical Creation accounts as a child in Sunday School. (Genesis 1:1-2:4, Genesis 2:5-24, and John 1:1-18). God's methodical work in each one is striking. God spoke each aspect into Being at the proper time with one aspect building upon the other, and then handed to the waters and the earth the final responsibility to "bring forth living creatures" (Genesis 1:20, 24).

I also knew that it was the same God of Creation in my Shawnee stories. God spoke Being into existence for the Jew. God simply thought Being into existence for the Shawnee. We Shawnee thus refer to God as the Most-Awesome-Mystery, which is similar to the Christian Godhead. We also think of God as the One-Who-Thinks-and-It-Happens. The traditional Shawnee speaks of God as Grandfather, which carries great respect in our culture.

Relationship With the Land

Most American Indian people think of self and the relationship with God in unison with the land and its interconnected communities. It is so with me as well. I was born on a farm in Muskingum County, OH, that had been home for my family for over 800 years. My family's oneness with the land could have ended with the Indian Removal Act of 1830, which required American

Indian populations of the east to move to reservations west of the Mississippi. However, three lines of my ancestry assumed white names to stay on the land. Neighbors perjured themselves by witnessing my ancestors' signatures on land purchased as "citizens." My family members donned white-man clothing, cut their hair, spoke English, and hid away or destroyed all that could identify them as Shawnee. They paid the price of their language, freedom of religion, artistic expression, and a culture of generosity so that they could stay on the land.

Creation Stories

As with many cultures, we have more than one creation story. Creation stories are neither systematic theology nor science. They attempt to grasp that which is beyond human comprehension. One Shawnee creation account explains the deep connection to the land that most American Indian cultures share.

When God created everything by thinking, God felt that there needed to be one creature that was intimate with God. Thus, God decided to make one creature out of the very Being of God. God took God's own heart, held it in God's hand, and cut it into many pieces. Then God threw the pieces to the four winds. The winds carried the pieces to the furthest points of the four directions and scattered them along the way. Wherever a heart-piece landed upon the earth, a new people sprang to life. God then spoke to each one through the heart, "Now you must learn about this place where you have fallen. Walk upon it. See it. Smell it. Taste it. Let it care for you. You care for it. You will learn the wisdom of this place. When you are ready, I will call you back to the Center where you will share your wisdom with the others who have learned from their places. As you share your wisdoms, you will join together, and you will restore the heart of God."

Through the elements of Creation God is intimately involved in each aspect of our being and living. Some speak of this intimacy as God breathing spirit into a being made of the earth. (Genesis 2) The earth and our place upon it, binds us to each other and to God. How can we know the names our children must have if they have not arisen from the land? How can we walk in harmony and beauty when we no longer can hear the land-rhythms that gave life to the songs? How can we know God when we cannot live where God commanded us to live for learning our part of God's wisdom to share with others? How can we truly be human when we are divided from the hearts of the land?

One Shawnee story relates that when humans first began walking upon the earth, they were pitiful beings. The animal-people asked God to make them more fit to walk upon God's earth. God replied that the animal-people could make the humans better by giving the humans their unique hearts. The wolf gave them a heart of family cooperation. The buffalo presented a heart of strength. The hawk shared a heart of patience. Each animal-person shared, and the humans became a little of each one's heart, each one's wisdom.

Yet the greatest gift awaited sharing. That gift came in response to human greed.

Humans combined the heart gifts from the animals and became greater than any one animal. Thus, humans could take what they wanted. God saw this and made a law that no human could take more than he could use and must give thanks for the life shared by the animal-people. Soon a human killed an animal without need, and he did not give thanks for its life, but nothing bad happened to him. The animal-people cried to God that there must be fairness. God gave the animal-people the gift of disease and poison to send among the humans until there was a balance. The animal-people were so angry they kept sending disease and poison when they should have stopped. The humans became fewer and weaker until they cried to God for a new fairness. The plant-people asked that they could be the fairness. Every disease or poison has a cure in the plants growing near to it. Humans continued to die, though, for none of them could speak the language of the plants. Only the animal-people could do that, and they were still angry and would not speak to the plant-people on behalf of the humans. The humans became so weak that all they could hunt were the children of the animal-people. It seemed that the humans would all die. Then one of the animal-people took pity upon them. Although they had killed her children and broken her heart, she took pity on them. She taught them the language of the plant-people. That animal-person was the bear. She continued to teach that if you want to heal your own broken heart, you first must forgive the ones who broke it. Then you not only will heal yourself, you will heal them as well.

Creation stories are powerful for they connect us to all of the forces of love and grace that caused God to bring forth Being. Animal-people gave their hearts away. Bear learned to forgive and heal. That power takes hold of the human heart once again in the telling of the stories. There is a healing of the present brokenness and a call to a renewed life in God through the stories of the creation.

Creation stories, finally, call us to love the Creation for the sake of the One who called it into existence. When the reality of God's gift finds lodging in our hearts, we will share our wisdoms in love and restore God's heart in a new heaven and a new earth.

Fred A. Shaw/Neeake
Shawandasse (Shawnee)
Retired Elder
West Ohio Conference

Questions for Discussion

1. How do you respond to the idea that Native Americans have their own Hebrew Bible (Old Testament) stories?
2. There is more than one creation story in the Bible. Is it possible for many creation stories from around the world to be true? Share why or why not.
3. A significant part of creation for Native Americans is relationship with the land. Based on your life experience, how do you view the earth and what is your relationship with it?
4. Fred Shaw describes creation as "the heart of God." How do you see creation as a reflection of the forces of love and grace from God?

Chapter 6

Worship

To worship is to lose oneself in the midst of communicating with the Great Mystery that is our God. For me, as a Native American Christian, worship engages my spirit in the prayer, praise, song, dance, sacrifice and thankfulness that mark my relationship with God as Father, Son and Holy Spirit.

Growing up in Oklahoma in the 50s and 60s, Christian worship meant that single hour of holding a square song book and sitting on a square pew in a square room, or at least that is the memory that remains for me from that period of my life.

Later, as the ways of Christian worship softened and eased up around the boundaries so that the sharp edges began to disappear, and new, more amorphous ways of powerful worship began to emerge, I found a place to experience a true communion with the Great Mystery within my United Methodist faith.

I also have memories from the early days of my life that include worship in places where I hear and see and touch running water; and in places where I see and feel the heat and flame of a sacred fire; and where I hear the sounds of songs in Cherokee and the beat of turtle shell shakers. There was such a total connection there between me as child of God, daughter of the community, and descendant of the path of my ancestors.

It took me a great number of years to figure out that both the Christian worship and the indigenous worship could co-exist within my world and within me. I am blessed now to walk with a sense of balance and cohesion, knowing that all the ways in which the Creator has come to me are connected in a sense of the unity of who I am.

It is important to understand that this feeling of unity is not a place where so many of my Native American brothers and sisters spiritually dwell. Because of historical trauma and the schizophrenia of the missionizing Christian denominations in this nation, many of my people are torn asunder by the unresolvable conflict within their souls. Being told that indigenous ways of worship were heathen and sinful, and that the alien experience of Christianity was the only legitimate way of knowing God, led to a kind of cultural schizophrenia that persists to the present day. It is a very real and present part of the historical trauma with which we live.

My co-author and friend, Henri, and I have engaged in many conversations about the brutal impact of the irreconcilable duality which so many of our people have been forced to experience. In the following essay, she shares much of herself and her Cheyenne ways of worship. I would point out to you as readers, that she honors you by sharing so much of herself in these words. Know that she considers you worthy of receiving great Truth.

Worship Where We Walk

The English word "worship," too, has its equivalent in indigenous languages, cultures, and thinking. As but one example, the Cheyenne call the annual solstice observance surrounding their two highest covenants ma'heónėstónestotse, "sacred ceremonies" or "sacred things." They also recognize Ma'heo'o "the sacred power, medicine, mystery," and they "think in a sacred way, or think spiritually" by following their traditional instructions. These ceremonials are reverential and as part of their devotional practice include prayer, fasting, sacrifice, ritual, song, and dance. Even the trees take part in ceremonies by serving as the center pole, marking the boundaries of sacred space, or providing a place in the sun and wind to tie offerings.

Sacred Elements of Worship

Worship in a Native American cultural context is done with an attitude of humility within a sacred space, on a mountain, at a sacred site, or at home, and it may be performed as a group or individually. The participant(s) makes an offering, such as tobacco, calico, food, or burns sweet grass or cedar sending the sacred smoke out to the four directions where the sacred powers of the world live and watch over creation.

Among the plains tribes, fasting can be either a group or individual ceremony, and may be done by either male or female. It is a testimony to individual strength and the ability to endure the elements of wind, rain, scorching heat by day, and bitter cold by night as the person further suffers by going without food and water for four days and nights. The person goes beyond self and his/her strength is a testimony to the individual's assurance and confidence in the power of the Creator or Great Mystery. It is a personal, extraordinary, indescribable, and life-altering worship experience.

The cloth ceremony is another culturally unique way of symbolizing the people's faith in the supreme ability of the Creator to heal and remove any illness or negativity from a person. Multiple pieces of cotton material, usually a yard in length, in colors associated with the four directions, such as white, red, yellow, and black or blue are knotted together in one corner and passed over an individual in a prescribed pattern by a person who has successfully fasted in one of the tribe's ceremonies. After this, they are tied to a tree at the people's sacred mountain or some designated outdoors area where the natural world participates in helping to maintain a people's health. The cloth used in this ceremony are oestónestotse, prayer cloths or offering cloths.

Thinking in a Sacred Way

In traditional thinking, Native Americans acknowledge the interdependent nature of the world with which they must live in reciprocity and mutuality in the food offerings ceremony. It is a thanksgiving that recognizes the gifts and kinship of the earth. Food offerings are respectfully made to each of the spirits of the four directions and then they are given to the earth, which acknowledges earth's sacredness. In the past, Cheyenne mothers used a phrase Ho'e é-ma'heóneve, through which they taught their children that earth is sacred and that all plants, animals, and all that exists in the earth circle of life are to be honored and respected. They must live lovingly in this world.

The first peoples of this land were and have always been spiritual thinkers, who think in a sacred way. For all time they have worshipped the Creator or Great Mystery, whose spirit fills the universe. They are a people who worship in the divine ways given them at Creation, in their own languages. Although they have oftentimes been mistreated and subjugated, they have never forgotten how to pray. Native peoples are prayerful and stated simply, they worship in perpetuity.

Dr. Henrietta Mann

An increasing number of contemporary Native Americans are blessing the rest of us by writing of their experience of walking in two worlds. One of these writers of sacred themes is Steve Barse. Steve is an award-winning author who, in addition to writing for the Native American Comprehensive Plan has written for the Upper Room. He is a tireless advocate for Native peoples in the Oklahoma City area. Steve shares with us his insight and introspection on the topic of worship.

Worship – A God-given Right Versus the Doctrine of Discovery

God is Spirit and those who worship him must worship in spirit and truth.
(John 4:24)

All the earth worships you; they sing praises to you, sing praises to
your name. Selah.
Psalms 66:4

The Doctrine of Discovery is the more than 500 year old claim that Christian empires had a divine right to appropriate whatever lands they "discovered." This notion was encouraged and spread by fifteenth-century popes to justify global land claims that came to include the Americas. Intentions were clear when popes of this era authorized Portugal and Spain in the conquest of "undiscovered" lands and the conversion or enslavement of the inhabitants, and the seizing of all lands and their resources. European explorers were sent to invade, search out, capture, vanquish, subdue and enslave the indigenous inhabitants of these "undiscovered" lands. Directives were soon issued to colonize the "new world." Thus the Doctrine of Discovery became the basis for centuries of colonization, oppression, slavery and genocide of the indigenous peoples of the world.

Freedom of Worship Under Assault

I equate worship to Indian prayer and ceremony. Indian ceremony came under full assault due to the insidiousness of the Doctrine of Discovery. This was addressed directly in the late 18th century by a Seneca tribal leader named Sa-Go-Ye-Ha, also known as Red Jacket. In research done by Rev. Glen "Chebon" Kernell, an elder in the Oklahoma Indian Missionary Conference, it was revealed that Red Jacket had a response to a request by the eighteenth-century European Christians who were trying to convert Native people. Red Jacket's analysis of the situation was,
You say that you are sent to instruct us how to worship the Great Spirit agreeably to his mind; and if we do not take hold of the religion which you white people teach, we shall be unhappy hereafter. You say that you are right and we are lost. How do you know this to be true? You say that there is but one way to worship and serve the Great Spirit. If there is but one religion, why do the white people differ so much from it? Why not all agree, as you all can read the book? We also have a religion that was handed to our forefathers, and has been handed down to us. We worship that way. The Great Spirit has made us all.

49

An eight-part documentary, 500 Nations, was released in 1995. Its intention was an exploration of the various Native American nations and their fall to the European conquerors—500 Nations, 500 languages, 500 world views, 500 creation stories, and 500 ways of worshiping. There is much to ponder here. It is a wonder that American Indians are not all raging alcoholics. That is not as provocative a statement as it may seem. The Europeans arrived and despite our best intentions to understand them, they set about taking away the most precious things in our lives. Our homelands, our languages, our children, and our adherence to the forms of worship the Creator gave us. Sadly, we were not brought the "good news." We were bought the bad news. Christian denominations were given full reign to enter Indian communities, most often with the full might of the United States military behind them. The intent was to crush our spirits along with our will to resist. We learned the word "heathen," and if we did not change we would be cast into a horrible place to burn forever. And many Indian people were left with the notion their belief system was evil.

The Power of Native Forms of Worship

Sweat lodge, the pipe, cedaring, the sacred arrows, the Lowampi ceremony—somehow, someway, and for some reason these forms of worship along with many, many others survived the devastation. In the twenty-first century, Indian people have inherited a spiritual legacy that has created doubt and mistrust. There has been much hurt, anger and frustration over the topic of "Indian Religion."

However, today there is a growing awareness that Indian ceremonies are indeed true and viable forms of worship. Before the first missionary set foot on this continent, our people had effectively sought out and communicated with God. He in turn blessed us with many forms of worship.

I would like to share two examples of the power of native forms of worship. The first example is from the Veterans Administration which actually sanctioned Native American ceremonial rites being held at a Vet Center in Oklahoma City for the healing of post traumatic stress disorder among vets. My brother, Harold Barse, was a VA Readjustment Counselor who used these ceremonial rites. He

50

spoke to the success of this program not only for Indian veterans, but non-Indians as well.

The second example is from my own experience within the sweat lodge. This rite brings together at one time all the elements that make up the human experience, the body, mind and spirit. The heat and steam cleanses and purifies the body. The isolation and darkness leave you free of distraction. And the shared intensity of group prayer brings you closer to the Creator. It can be a deeply satisfying and meaningful worship experience.

The Kiowa ethos and culture is captured in the mythic being of Saynday, the tribe's trickster character. Many tribes have trickster figures in their traditional stories. Through their sometimes foolish and funny or sometimes wise and heroic ways, the trickster teaches the tribal community the lessons of life. He was sent to earth by the Great Mystery, and his survival and that of the tribe often depended on cunning, cleverness, prowess, and a shrewd ability to do the right thing at the right time. These traits became the shared values of the tribe and brought meaning to everyday life. But sadly, Saynday developed a dual personality. He had brought the Kiowa people from underneath the earth and into a world of light. He brought them through many difficult times. Yet, he developed a trickster side that brought him—and the tribe—agony and embarrassment. This Saynday mirrored the disintegration of the world the Kiowa people once knew. This is a fair description of historical (or generational) trauma.

Through exposure to others and a willingness to learn I have come to understand the relevance and power of our ceremonies and worship, particularly for these troubling times. I have come to believe that American Indians have a great deal to share with the world, and someday soon we will have the opportunity to do so.

Steve Barse
Kiowa
First American United Methodist Church, Norman, OK
Oklahoma Indian Missionary Conference

Questions for Discussion

1. What similarities can you find between the forms of Native American worship of which Henri writes and your Christian ways of worship?
2. As a Native American person, how have you had to reconcile your Native beliefs with your Christian beliefs?
3. How has the Doctrine of Discovery impacted your life?
4. When, within your experience of worship, whether Native American or Christian or both, have you felt closest to God?

Chapter 7

History

My family still lives on a small piece of our original allotment land. In the 1887 Dawes Act, the lands where many Native nations had lived for endless generations or where other nations had settled as a result of government treaty, suddenly became property to be divided into allotments for individual families. The intent was to "civilize" Native peoples into being individual land owners, thus undermining tribal identity and existence, and to open the vast unalloted sections of land to white settlers.

In the case of the Cherokee people who were one of many tribes forced into Oklahoma Territory on Trails of Tears, the location where we received our allotments was in far northeastern Oklahoma. It is a wooded area with adequate fresh water, rolling hills and low mountain ridges. When I am driving through my home community in Oklahoma, I sometimes try to imagine what my ancestors felt when they first looked upon the land there. I pray that they were comforted by the beautiful landscapes.

Not all tribes that were forced into Oklahoma Territory were as fortunate as mine was. I recall a time when I served as a district superintendent for the Southern District of my conference, the Oklahoma Indian Missionary Conference. I was at a church meeting in the southwest part of Oklahoma. The nations in that part of OIMC came from the central and southern plains and were migratory peoples for the most part. I found myself sitting with a woman elder from the church. She asked about my tribe and where I lived. When I shared my response with her, she looked off as into the distance and said "You come from a beautiful, green place. We were not so fortunate. When they got to us, all that was left was this dry and dusty place. But we love it now. It is our home." I believe her statement is a testimony to several things, one is the deep love that Native peoples hold for the land—even a harsh land draws our love and devotion; a second is the haphazard kinds of factors that influenced the totality of our lives. It could as easily have been my nation allotted to live in hard places—in fact my family's land is rocky and hard to farm. And third, our history is always tied to the land. I believe this is a distinction that sets Native Americans apart from other folks in this country.

When I look across the five acres where I live, I remember all that my people were forced to endure and I realize that I stand on holy ground—the so-called reparations for generations of suffering. The history that led to me alive at this place and time is a part of my inheritance and it is with me every day. Many of the Cherokee people forced on the death march to Oklahoma were Christian. Cherokee hymns were sung along that awful trail, many of which are still sung today. We believe the Creator walked with us throughout our history and still walks with us.

Henri has spoken to me about the Sand Creek Massacre which is such an important part of her people's history. As she related the details of that dreadful day, I could hear her ancestors speaking through her. I felt the terror of that attack and the shock and grief that followed. Clearly, for Henri this episode of history is not an event recorded on a page in a book that sits on a shelf, waiting to be opened. She carries it in her heart and has passed the truth of it to her descendants. I was honored that she shared the story with me.

Our Very Present History

Native Americans have lived long on this land, and the stories of their beginnings postulate they were created here or came from the stars, sky land above, or from worlds below. They spoke unique languages which reflected their cultural diversity. They evolved their distinct cultures as they walked the Road of Life that extends from creation to today and into an infinite future. These early philosophers measured time by the seasons and the position of the sun, moon, and the constellations. Some of them also utilized counting sticks or sticks they notched with each passing day. They were history-makers, storing their histories and traditional knowledge in their hearts and minds, which they passed down verbally from one generation to the next.

Desperate History

Following 1492, however, the native world changed forever when Christopher Columbus accidently sailed into this hemisphere and tragically ushered in the American Indian holocaust and practice of genocide. Estimates of the native population in North America at contact range from a conservative 1 million upward to noted anthropologist Russell Thornton's adjusted count of 5.65 million, to other estimates of even higher numbers. Regardless of population, however, by 1890 when all American Indians were first included in the federal census they numbered 250,000. Their depopulation was the result of conflict; holocaust that included the burning of the inhabitants of some of the Pequot praying towns; diseases—key among them smallpox and measles; manifest destiny; and American cultural imperialism.

Christopher Columbus was operating under international legal law, the so-called Doctrine of Discovery, which in this case served as justification for gaining possession of Native American homelands. After the adoption of the United States Constitution in 1789 and until 1871, treaties with the various American Indian nations provided for huge land cessions, which ultimately left native people with but a small land base. The prevailing nineteenth-century philosophy of Manifest Destiny as a divinely ordained right, resulted in the expansion and settlement of the continent from the Atlantic seaboard to the Pacific Ocean, which further eroded the already decreased Indian landholdings.

Other tribes were displaced or relocated, and the Federal government eventually codified its removal policy in the 1830 Removal Act. Some 16,000 Cherokee were forcefully removed from their Eastern homelands to Indian Territory and 4,000 of them perished along the way. They call this forced march "The Trail Where

55

They Cried." Other tribes cried as they, too, were literally herded from the South, West, and North into the current State of Oklahoma, which was initially slated to become an Indian state. Genocide and holocaust were the by-products of governmental policy, which sanctioned greed for the land and dispossessed native peoples.

Sand Creek and the Washita River

The events behind the settlement of the Cheyenne and Arapaho in Oklahoma are tragic. They had negotiated a small reservation in southeastern Colorado Territory in the 1861 Treaty of Fort Wise. Anti-Indian sentiment ran high and the settlers wanted Indian title extinguished. A militia was organized; a Methodist lay minister by the name of John M. Chivington was placed in charge; and on the bitterly cold dawn of November 29, 1864 attacked the sleeping encampment of Black Kettle, Cheyenne, and Left Hand, Arapaho. The atrocities committed by Chivington and his men were horrific and resulted in three Congressional and military hearings. Chivington was found guilty but never punished and to his dying day stood by his actions at Sand Creek.

Over a century later, the 1996 General Conference of The United Methodist Church apologized to the Cheyenne and Arapaho for the actions of one of their clergy at Sand Creek, which set a new direction in church and tribal relations. Sand Creek is but one more example of how Indians were dealt with in as much as they were viewed as obstacles to progress and Manifest Destiny. For the Cheyenne the nightmare of Sand Creek was to be repeated four years later this time along the Washita River.

Black Kettle, acknowledged as the most peaceable of all Cheyenne peace chiefs, took his band south into Indian Territory away from those seeking revenge for Sand Creek. He signed the 1867 Treaty of Medicine Lodge, which contained a compulsory education provision. Before they reported to the agency, almost four years to the day after Sand Creek, another pre-dawn attack was carried out by George Armstrong Custer and his men of the 7th Cavalry along the Washita River. Black Kettle and his wife were killed trying to cross the frozen river. All the personal possessions left by the

Cheyenne as they fled were burned; 52 hostages were taken; and the entire pony herd of 875 was killed in a virtual shooting frenzy. This unforeseen winter attack had the desired effect.

Christian Denominations and Boarding Schools

Like other tribes, the Cheyenne and Arapaho eventually reported to the reservation and reluctantly took up the different ways of life imposed upon them. Their children filtered in to the Euro-American English-only schools on the reservation, which were called manual labor or industrial training schools. The federal government had instituted new policy by delegating responsibility for Indian Affairs to the various Christian denominations.

The American Society of Friends or Quakers were put in charge of the Cheyenne and Arapaho Reservation. Their "civilizing," educational, and Christianizing work was eventually shared by the Mennonites. In 1871 Arapaho children were the first to attend the Quaker-operated schools because Chief Little Raven stated they had to leave the "Buffalo Road" and follow the "Corn Road." It was not until 1875 that the Cheyenne as a tribe sent their children to school.

In 1879 off-reservation boarding schools were established and some Indian children were taken from their families and sent to these schools far from home. Carlisle Indian Industrial Training School in Pennsylvania operated by Richard Henry Pratt was the first such school. The curriculum in these off-reservation schools, like those on reservations, consisted of religious instruction, a basic English education, and vocational instruction. Focused upon assimilation and producing white Anglo Saxon Protestant citizens, it was their avowed intent to "Kill the Indian and Save the Man."

This forced eradication of culture and genocide in military encounters such as the Trail of Tears, Sand Creek, and the Washita have had horrendous psychological effect upon Native Americans. They have been subjected to three powerful institutions: the Federal government, church, and education. Tragically, the intergenerational effect can be seen and felt in many native communities and is referred to as historical trauma or historical grief. After World War II the United States of America developed the Marshall Plan to rebuild war-torn Germany. Native Americans suffered the same experience, but there has been no government plan to rebuild their nations, and historical trauma remains a continuing issue.

Dr. Henrietta Mann

Two decades ago David Wilson and I wrote a play about the history of the Oklahoma Indian Missionary Conference. At the time we were both seminary students. The play was written on the occasion of the Sesquicentennial Celebration of OIMC (150 year anniversary). As part of our research we examined the histories of many tribes who came to Oklahoma (Indian Territory). We learned about the journeys of so many of our sister tribes throughout Oklahoma, how they managed to survive the genocide and came through the fire.

In hindsight, it feels that our Creator helped prepare David and myself for the ways we would serve our people within The United Methodist Church. As the Conference Superintendant for OIMC, David travels across the entire conference which extends from northeastern Kansas through Oklahoma and into north Texas. Because he has claimed the many tribes of OIMC as his peoples, he is always with family. David is the grandson of an original Choctaw Code-Talker from World War I. He participates in many cultural activities including Gourd Dance, pow wows, Native American sweat lodge, and many other tribal organizations and activities. Here, David writes of the history of his people and of all Native Americans.

History in the Eyes of Native Americans

It is impossible for any Native American person to write a comprehensive history of our peoples. At last count, there were over 550 tribes across this country, each with their own individual stories that tell of their past and present. The unfortunate reality is that one person can read or hear the history of a single tribe or nation and assume that it is the history of all native people. That is not the case.

I will attempt to write about the understanding of history in the eyes of many Native American people, both individual and corporate. I also write from the perspective of a Native person who has been raised in the United Methodist Church since childhood.

Choctaws and Christianity in Oklahoma

I am a member of the Choctaw Tribe which was Christianized in the late 1700's and early 1800's by the Methodists, Presbyterians and others. Many of the Choctaw people accepted this new religion because it was so similar to what their Native spirituality taught – basic precepts to treat each other with respect and love.

When the U.S. government forcibly removed our people to what is now the state of Oklahoma, the Choctaw people brought Christianity with them, most notably, Methodism. One of the first things the Choctaws did in this new land was to set up Methodist churches in Southeast Oklahoma. They were the first to set up Methodist churches in that part of Indian Territory and I remind Methodists all over the state of Oklahoma that the Oklahoma Indian Missionary Conference (OIMC) is the mother church of Methodism in Oklahoma. We brought Methodism to Oklahoma on our Trail of Tears. Churches and communities all over the state carry those stories today. And it isn't just a story, but a significant part of our history in which we can say, despite the suffering and tragedy of the past, we brought the gospel of Jesus Christ to this new land.

Living Histories

I have the pleasure of being able to travel to the Native American United Methodist churches in OIMC and I continue to learn about the lives of our people as both Christians and tribal nations. One thing I realized was while most Americans consider history to be a recounting of events from the past, only to be remembered in text books, history is a living mechanism for Native peoples. Typically, we do not speak of our present life without referring to events and persons of the past. These past events and persons help define who we are today.

For example, many have heard of the Sand Creek Massacre of 1864, a tragic event wherein a Methodist preacher in Colorado led a regiment of militia to attack a peaceful Native American village. The village, flying the American flag and the white flag of truce. had been told they were under the protection of the U.S. Military. However, Colonel John Chivington and his troops massacred over 200 Cheyenne and Arapaho people, mostly women, children and the elderly. This story has been shared at the United Methodist General Conference and in stories offered to the church.

When I attend various powwows or dances in Oklahoma, the women will be wearing beautiful shawls of various designs and patterns. Some shawls carry appliquéd symbols from tribal groups or organizations and often there will be wording across the back of the shawls. From time to time, I see a shawl with the words, "Sand Creek Massacre Descendants." These persons are direct descendants of that event and that history is a very present part of who they are.

For many, this historical atrocity is simply an event from the past. For the people directly affected by this massacre, it is a living thing. Not that Native people hang on to the past, but we understand that these events help to define us and to enable us to be proud of our ancestors who fought hard to do what was right. Our history is also a reminder of the strength that we draw from our ancestors who sacrificed so much for this generation.

Oral History Remains with Us

An unfortunate fact to remember when reading the histories of Native peoples is that the majority of what is written comes from non-Native persons, and the written content may tell more about the perspective of the author than it does about the subjects. If our histories are told, they are often romanticized, or mentioned only briefly. I often found myself telling the history of OIMC in seminary classes because the professors did not know the stories. It is the same for students who attend pastors' Course of Study School and other continuing education events. We often bring up our Native histories because others do not. And many times, students or peers will ask,

"Did that really happen?" Perhaps it is the guilt they feel or their unwillingness to believe that Christian people could have treated Native people so terribly throughout the past.

Fortunately for us, our histories have been passed down from generation to generation. Native peoples are of an oral tradition. Although the Internet and social media are now being used in an effort to preserve our languages and stories, for the most part, we still learn them from our elders, our parents and grandparents. These are stories that come to us with the expectation of being passed to the next generation.

History Passed from our Elders

My predecessor, the late Rev. Dr. Thomas Roughface of the Ponca Tribe was someone very well known for the wealth of information that he carried. It was not just information he had learned in the classroom, but mostly the stories, songs and histories he had learned from his parents, grandparents and fellow tribal peoples. I was thankful we had been able to record stories and songs on tape and video before his passing.

When he was serving as Conference Superintendent, I would go to him often with questions about local churches and people in OIMC. I learned quickly that his responses were not brief and often he would not directly answer my questions. Instead, his responses would be stories of the past, related to my question. It was important for him to pass along what he felt was pertinent about persons and events that shaped local churches and our conference. His responses would often take half an hour or longer. I would always make sure that I had enough time to listen to his responses.

Most important, after his passing, I was truly grateful for the information he passed along to me and many others. This is a difficult concept for dominant American culture to understand, because persons do not take enough time to stop and listen. In this world of ever-increasing technology and access to information, I often wonder about our future. We must not only learn by memorization, but truly hear the stories that our elders are so willing to share. It is important to understand that our elders are willing to share these stories with all people who truly want to listen and understand who we are. I have found that the majority of Native persons are willing to share their stories and histories, but often are not asked.

One of my favorite scripture passages is found in Hebrews 13:7. The author writes, "Remember your leaders, those who spoke the word of God to you; consider the outcome of their way of life, and imitate their faith." These words are a reminder about the living histories from our past—the stories that have shaped us as God's people, and helped us to shape others' lives into the future.

Rev. Dr. David Wilson
Choctaw
Conference Superintendant
Oklahoma Indian Missionary Conference

Questions for Discussion

1. Within your personal and/or family identity does history play a significant part? Why or why not?
2. Is it possible to forgive genocidal actions against a whole people? Why or why not?
3. In your experience, what role do Native Americans play in the history of Christianity in this country or in the history of Methodism in this country?
4. Share with one another a story which is important to your family, church or tribal history.

Chapter 8

Justice

For Native American Christians, we celebrate that Jesus was a tribal man who honored his traditions and took part in his ceremonial rites; and we celebrate that justice was a matter of primary concern in his ministry on earth.

One of the most challenging aspects of living life as an indigenous person is carrying within us the experiences of injustice from the past and the present. Knowing that my grandmothers and grandfathers were forced to leave behind their homes in North Carolina and Georgia and other parts of the Southeast simply because someone coveted their land and possessions is a hard and dreadful truth. Knowing that so many of my people perished on those terrible death marches is impossible to live with outside the grace of Jesus Christ. Knowing that my children and grandchildren are facing issues like law enforcement profiling; land, water and natural resource theft; extreme levels of prison incarceration; historical trauma and so much more is excruciating and unbearable outside the hope of Jesus Christ. These are matters of injustice.

Henri has shared the terrible reality of how her people have suffered unjustly in the past and how they face continued injustice today. She has also shared about the gifts given by the Great Mystery that help to bring hope and vision to the Cheyenne and Arapaho people. In this essay she talks about justice, and the struggle to achieve it for Native Americans.

Justice – A Community Value

From a traditional and historical perspective, the majority of the first peoples' of this land lived in just communities that were governed by strong values, which emphasized the development of good character and proper and balanced relationships. Such values encouraged ethical behavior with a strong sense of right or wrong, which were successful in keeping conflict to a minimum. Among those values was and still is respect, the positive esteem and consideration that a person accords all life.

Respect appears to no longer have much relevance judging from the rampant injustice that exists on many fronts, ranging from blatant human rights violations to alarming environmental justice issues. Despite the fact that native peoples live in a relational world in which everything is seen as being related and which necessitates that everyone stand in proper relationship with everyone and everything else, there appears to be no acknowledgement of relationship and kinship in dominant society.

After 1492

Kinship is supposed to bind, yet people and nations adhere to their distinct world views, which appear to have no latitude for compromise. Unfortunately, after 1492 and following Anglo European contact, Native Americans became an oppressed peoples and serve as the nation's miners' canary. As a result, they confront a range of justice issues, and land is critical among them. The majority of American Indians traditionally have a sacred interdependent relationship with the land, which many view as their spiritual Mother. Most Euro-Americans subscribe to the concept of Manifest Destiny which they believe grants them the divine authority to exert dominion over everything on planet earth. Thus, land became a contentious justice issue virtually at contact.

Land cessions became the standard in Indian-U.S. treaties along with pledges of perpetual peace and friendship. Acknowledged as sovereign nations in the treaty-making process, Indians reserved for themselves certain rights, and usually smaller tracts of often less desirable lands. In exchange for land, the Federal government agreed to provide certain annuities, rations, and services. Of the more than 400 treaties, 371 were ratified by the United States Senate, and are considered by the U.S. Constitution to be "the supreme Law of the Land."

Notwithstanding the high legal standing of treaties, most, if not all, Indian-U.S. treaties have been violated by the Federal government. Another critical situation of injustice is the lack of protection for Indian sacred sites. American Indians have a unique relationship with the land/earth for which they are responsible. They go to their sacred sites to pray, make offerings, renew themselves, seek spiritual guidance and direction, and for some to observe world renewal ceremonies. It is oftentimes difficult to access these Indian sacred places or protect them from development, since an approximate 75 percent of them are on Federal lands.

Justice as Religious Freedom and Claiming Ancestral Remains

In 1978, the Congress passed the American Indian Religious Freedom Act (AIRFA) as a joint resolution of Congress, and its passage leads one to question the effectiveness of freedoms enshrined in the First Amendment. The report mandated by AIRFA documented over 500 incidents of government infringements on American Indian religious freedom, and listed nearly forty pages of recommendations for administrative changes and legislative remedies. The 1990 Native American Graves Protection and Repatriation Act (NAGPRA) was a direct outcome of the AIRFA report.

NAGPRA is the federal legislation that mandates the repatriation of artifacts, sacred objects, cultural patrimony, and most importantly more than 300,000 ancestral human remains that are warehoused in museums throughout the country. The process of return has been slow and has been hampered by the requisite research and documentation required for their return. NAGPRA addresses a religious and human rights violation, which is a blatant issue of justice.

Another justice issue is the "repatriation" of native languages, which historically were slated for eradication. Fortunately, they were resistant and several hundred survived the linguistic holocaust, but many of them are now on the brink of extinction. Native language eradication can be traced to an educational system of primarily industrial training/boarding schools that worked hand in glove with the churches and Federal government in the destruction of these first languages.

A Way to Resolve Conflict Justly

With justice issues of such magnitude, it is important to utilize mechanisms to address the sources of conflict they create within native communities. A talking circle is a tool for addressing such individual and community imbalance. The people sit in a circle and may initially purify themselves with sweet grass to put them in the proper frame of mind. A person who wishes to speak takes and holds a talking stick and everyone listens intently and respectfully with no interruptions. The talking stick is passed to another speaker who may offer an additional solution or comment. Other solutions are put forth which are discussed until consensus is reached. Ultimately, the solution represents the collective wisdom of those assembled who have worked to resolve conflict, and the solution is passed on for action and implementation. Talking circles are traditional and effective ways of minimizing conflict.

Dr. Henrietta Mann

Marcus Briggs-Cloud has accomplished much for a person of any age. So it is especially exciting to learn that he is a young adult. I have had the privilege of experiencing his musical talent at annual conference and was not surprised to learn that Marcus has been nominated for a Grammy award for his Native American music in the Maskoke language.

An instructor at the Muscogee Nation Tribal College and lecturer on his tribal traditions, Marcus contributes to the hope for justice and balance in the world. In the following essay, he offers to us reason for measured optimism in the search for justice.

God's Call to Do Justice

I vividly remember sitting in an auditorium at the 2007 United Methodist Student Movement Forum awaiting a speaker to arrive and address those gathered on the topic of indigenous justice. As moments rolled on, several persons attempted to stimulate dialogue around the scheduled theme, when one student blurted out "there are three Native Americans sitting in the back....let them speak." My peers pushed me forward, stating I would be the "spokesperson." I hesitantly approached the front of the room, quickly calling to mind a responsibility from my ancestors to speak about every injustice I could recall that had been experienced by my People. These injustices ranged from displacement and genocide to environmental racism and negative stereotype imagery in media and sports. I envisioned sharing stories of our children who were abducted from their homes and placed in church and government run boarding schools. In these schools, children were severely abused for speaking their own languages or displaying any form of their Indigenous identities. And of course, I could not exclude contemporary issues such as highest rates of drug abuse, domestic violence, alcoholism and suicide – all emerging from historical trauma and other components of colonization that have generationally infected and fragmented our communities. To my surprise, the only words to come forth from my mouth were from Micah 6:8,

What does the Lord require of you, but to do justice,
and to love kindness, and to walk humbly with your God."
(Micah 6:8)

During that time in my life, I grappled intensely with theological mysteries while comparing and contrasting Christian ways with those of my own Maskoke People. However, as I uttered the scripture from Micah, those intellectual and spiritual challenges were in an instant collapsed into an ironic but potentially complimentary relationship between the uncountable acts of injustice

67

done to Native Americans, and God's call to do justice. This pivotal moment revealed to me a question relating to the tangled connection between two traditions which emerged from vastly different geographic places, traditions that seemed impossible to reconcile. The question was, if we stood on the common ground of doing justice in God's world, how could our Native American and Euro-American traditions contribute to the Church of Jesus Christ? And, additionally, how can Indigenous contributions to the Church help reinvigorate, reshape and strengthen Indigenous traditions in our own contexts and communities?

Including Indigenous Voices

There are many ways to approach this possibility, but the inner workings of the Church is undoubtedly a good starting point—a place where Indigenous Peoples have historically not been invited or welcomed, thus allowing little contribution from Native spirituality at the table of theological development. In my experience in the global church, Indigenous "inclusivity" has often been reduced to merely tolerating, showcasing, or sometimes even appreciating song and dance, waving a feather and burning some sage in a designated space. Justice in the Church for Indigenous Peoples must go beyond these safe zone practices which are often used in ways disrespectful to sacred origins. Notably, cultural integrity and respect for God-given differences become lost in attempting to justify indigenous sacred rites and ceremonies through the lens of Christianity. The fear of being labeled pagan by those Christians who still operate out of European missionary mindsets remains a threat to many.

Seeking justice rather, involves first affirming traditional Indigenous beliefs about the origins of the universe, creation stories, the nature of gender and kinship structures and other philosophical frameworks that Indigenous Peoples have maintained through communication with the sacred, even prior to colonization. We must acknowledge and remain content in admitting that we need not impose a claim that Indigenous and Christian traditions are somehow "the same" in order to justify the practice of one to the other. Rather, acknowledging their unique path of development as both being products of revelation from the sacred, is perhaps the most just avenue on which to embark.

Lenses of Justice

One of my favorite scripture verses that invokes potential liberation and healing from ongoing injustices penetrating the lives of my People, is Matthew 6:10,

Your kingdom come. Your will be done, on earth as it is in heaven.
(Matthew 6:10)

Feminist theology has taught us that the Greek word *basileia* (βασιλεία), usually translated "kingdom" in English biblical scriptures actually refers to ruling in general, regardless of gender and thus may be translated as the "realm of God." Applying this kind of lens to scripture is indeed enacting justice considering my own cultural context—the Maskoke People, a traditionally matriarchal society, which has been victimized by male domination and the subsequent rise of domestic violence. This verse is the ultimate call to do justice by bringing the realm of God to earth which may include living sustainably in accordance with mother earth, buying fair trade coffee, fighting English-only mentality and unjust immigration policies on lands that inherently belong to Indigenous Peoples.

Making Right the Imbalances

A word for justice and similar concepts do not exist in my own Maskoke language and society, since annual renewal ceremonies during the summer season make right all imbalances between and among those who operate within that ceremonial space. These renewal ceremonies engage members of the community in rites of regeneration and restoration. This does, however, present a problem when considering the attempt to seek justice between Maskoke People and those who operate outside of our ceremonial spaces who have committed injustice. Many Indigenous societies have similar renewal ceremonies that involve forms of reconciliation, an act of seeking justice, but are inclusive of only those who operate communally within that particular ceremonial society. Thus, while the Church bears responsibility in the dismantling and destruction of Indigenous societies, it also offers new ground for our Peoples to stand on by naming this concept of justice that our ancestors did not name separately from everyday life. It provides us with a vocabulary and a place to discuss issues of injustice, and a way to confront those who perpetrate injustice. Granted, the church is not the only place to find such discussions, since traditional Indigenous Peoples are also engaging the conversation. But, it is a place to begin doing justice in communion with our neighbors who still reside in our lands and must come to know more about our ways, as we continue our long time knowledge of theirs.

Kvnfvske Yvholv Marcus Briggs-Cloud
Maskoke Nation
First American United Methodist Church, Norman, OK
Oklahoma Indian Missionary Conference

Questions for Discussion

1. What are some examples of injustice from your family or tribal history?
2. What has helped you live with the knowledge of serious injustice from your own, your family's and/or your tribe's past?
3. Do you think use of the talking circle and talking stick could be used in situations of conflict with which you are familiar? Why or why not?
4. Marcus Briggs-Cloud asks the question, If we stood on the common ground of doing justice in God's world, how could our Native American and Euro-American traditions contribute to the Church of Jesus Christ? How would you answer this question?

Chapter 9

The Earth

There is a sacred quality that surrounds our Mother Earth. It is always present, but most of the time we tune it out. I have a Native American friend who once told me the earth helped to heal him from the grief of losing a son—his healing was not from a distance, but rather he felt compelled to physically let the earth hold him. He went to a quiet, wooded, holy place and lay down in a buckled place in the earth. He literally felt himself being held and healed.

In my walk of faith I have also experienced literal healing through Mother Earth. The Keetoowah Cherokee have holy ceremonial grounds where elements of fire and water call us to actions of worship. Medicine people use the bits and pieces of earth in healing ways. I have been witness to miraculous healings. There is tremendous power for good from Mother Earth.

My friend, Henri, is a respectful and caring daughter of Mother Earth. She has sacred sites for her people which she periodically visits. There is an exchange of energy which takes place. Henri offers all the respect and obedience of a beloved child and the Earth offers spiritual and physical renewal to her children. The Creator has designed a wonderful system and flow between Mother Earth and those who understand and appreciate her.

The following essay reflects Henri's great love and concern for Mother Earth. It also demands that we appreciate the way our actions impact the Earth and that we accept the responsibility for what we do to her.

The Sacred Earth

This earth, variously referred to as soil, ground, land, or the world, is the beloved planetary home of nearly seven billion human beings. Native Americans number around two million or as many as four million if one includes those that are Native American combined with some other nationality. Although their numbers were substantially decreased following Anglo European contact, by virtue of being this country's oldest people, they are its grandparent generation. As loving grandparents, they possess great wisdom, and foremost is their recognition of the interdependent nature of life, wherein all life forms depend upon other life forms for existence.

Native cultures and their diverse ways of life have grown from the very soil of this land. Traditional knowledge is rooted in the earth that sustains and nourishes them as a mother does her children, the analogy of which has its basis in many of their origin stories. In one such account, Creator decreed Planet Earth to be the most beautiful of the entire creation, and was to be known as Grandmother, first Mother and oldest woman. Human beings, her children, were to keep her company and live harmoniously on her as good caretakers of Earth.

The Circle of the Earth

Their lengthy land tenure has resulted in the development of sophisticated native philosophies, one of which is the circle which illustrates the earth or world and the road of life. The circle can be divided into quadrants with each quarter symbolizing different life aspects, such as age, age-related responsibility, seasons of the year, color, or direction. There is a resultant emphasis upon the four directions from which come the winds. Each quadrant is associated with the development of certain attributes, such as gentleness, strength, perseverance, and wisdom. This native concept was developed independent of astronomy whose symbol for earth is described as a cross within a circle, which is identical to the native circle of life.

To Native Americans the circle is sacred and so is Earth. Thus, the people exist as co-equal beings in a sacred landscape, which has certain places where spiritual power is concentrated. As conscientious stewards, they have a reciprocal and interdependent relationship with those sacred places, where they must observe prescribed rituals. Consequently, they must make pilgrimages to these sacred places time and again as a way of giving back to the Earth. They must go to these specific sites to observe their ceremonies and offer prayers and song that are necessary for maintaining the delicate balance of the world and for strengthening the spirit of all people. They are places that continue to guide the spiritual life and the hearts and minds of the people. They are places where individuals fast or give thanks. They may be world renewal sites, which necessitate periodic ceremonies to restore the health of the earth and all that exists upon it. Earth is the peoples' altar from which their prayers go out to Creator and to the four directions. Native spirituality has withstood the test of time and the people have kept their promises of principled stewardship. They are earth born and earth bound in a respectful relationship as the keeper people of Earth.

Water is Life and Life is Water

In addition to land, the Earth's surface is approximately 71% salt water oceans. Earth's oceans have a strong relationship to the moon, Earth's satellite. Commonly called Grandmother Moon, she not only exerts a strong influence upon the ocean tides, but upon the cycles of women, as well. This "night sun" is celebrated in ceremony, and native people love her, just as they do the sun, and other stars.

The grandparents are seriously concerned about the future of their grandchildren, especially when it comes to water. To them, water is life and life is water. Drinkable water is becoming more precious and one day it could become more valuable than gold. Some human beings have strayed far from the spiritual center and have seemingly lost their humanity. They are governed by economic greed.

Sanctity of the Earth is Challenged

Corporate America has desecrated the Earth primarily by extracting non-renewable fossil fuels such as gas and oil in its thirst for energy and money. The unfortunate oil catastrophe in the Gulf of Mexico should have been quickly addressed to mitigate its disastrous effects upon the water and plant people, and tribes. In addition, the nation's scientific community has violated Earth's sanctity in many ways but primarily by underground nuclear testing. Now, it is concerned about where in the earth they can safely store hazardous waste.

The nation's rivers and streams are polluted, as are the oceans. The air is contaminated and the clouds drop acid rain. The seeds of the plant people are being genetically altered. The Earth's biodiversity is threatened. Native languages are at risk of disappearing forever. Earth's inhabitants face the dangers associated with climate change and global warming, and they must become environmentally conscious. The grandparents have every reason to fear for the future of their grandchildren.

Dr. Henrietta Mann

Thom White Wolf Fassett is a shining star within our community. We long to see our Native American people represented among the leadership of The United Methodist Church and Brother Thom served as General Secretary for the General Board of Church and Society. However, from his humble and modest ways, you would never know this.

He is also the author of Giving Our Hearts Away: Native American Survival which was the text book for the UMW School of Mission Study on Native Americans. We are so proud of him. Here, Thom writes of biblical stones and Indian stones and all kinds of stones, and gives us something deep to think about.

The Earth: Living Stones

The very stones will cry out from the wall,
and the plaster will respond from the woodwork.
(Habakkuk 2:11)

Bear fruits worthy of repentance. Do not begin to say to
yourselves, 'We have Abraham as our ancestor' for I tell you, God is
able from these stones to raise up children to Abraham.
(Luke 3:8)

Some of the Pharisees in the crowd said to him, 'Teacher, order your
disciples to stop.' He answered, 'I tell you, if these were silent, the
stones would shout out.'
(Luke 19:39-40)

Come to him, a living stone, though rejected by mortals yet chosen
and precious in God's sight, and like living stones, let yourselves be
built into a spiritual house, to be a holy priesthood, to offer spiritual
sacrifices acceptable to God through Jesus Christ.
(1 Peter 2:5)

What are we to make of stones in this age of human beings
who seem to live so distant from the earth? It was clear that the
early people of the Old Testament were familiar with the images
of stones and even talked about their power. And then, in the New
Testament, we find even more powerful statements about stones
spoken by people who lived hundreds of years later. And even Jesus,
it is clear, had a working understanding of stones. I don't think we
are talking about magic stones or special stones. We are just talking
about every day stones found everywhere.

The First Things of Creation

Some of us have learned from our parents or grandparents or
our traditions about stones and rocks. In some of our traditions, we
know that they are recognized as the first things of creation. They
are the first forms fashioned by the creator. Some of our traditions

even attribute these stones as having been alive, creatures of the new creation. It's difficult to grasp these teachings because of our modern life-styles distracting us from the original teachings as we get caught up in consumerism and computers and scientific technology and making money to live. And some would even question us if we seemed to have an unusual interest in stones as symbols of meaning or representing stories and truths that could not be learned in any other way.

The scriptures seem to be telling us that ancient wisdom about stones is not unusual and doesn't seem to change from generation to generation. After all, "God is able from these stones to raise up children to Abraham." Even Jesus knew about them when he was met with resistance to his disciples' teaching and said, "I tell you, if these were silent, the stones would shout out." And in the 1 Peter reference, Jesus was considered a living stone and we—through the scripture—are challenged to become living stones allowing ourselves to be built into spiritual houses, a holy priesthood.

A Pile of Stones

My father, Spotted Horse, was a traditional Lakota pipe-carrier from the Standing Rock Reservation in South Dakota. By John Wayne's standards, he was a medicine man. And, although my mother was Seneca, there were common stories and traditions and oral stories that I knew about. But I didn't know much about stones. I had read the biblical accounts as we are looking at them now but never saw more deeply than what was obvious. One day, after a long-delayed visit to my father, we sat in his little one-room house on the Sitting Bull camp on the Grand River making what he called cowboy coffee and talking. Making the coffee was an important social ritual for him and he threw a fistful of coffee into a pot of water and put it on the propane hot plate to boil. He had no electricity. Once it finished boiling and the churning grounds settled to the bottom, he poured a cup for each of us. I choked down the black water out of respect for him and listened to one of his rodeo stories.

As we sat at his little table by the open door where the light could brighten the room, I noticed a pile of stones outside of the door. They were not big stones but ones that you could put in your pocket or carry in a bag. I asked him what they were for. He shifted in his chair and his face visibly changed as he prepared himself to tell me something. "Well," he said reaching for the handful of stones on the little table where we sat, "people bring me stones." I asked him what he did with them. He cleared his throat a few times and said, "People bring them to me from miles around. They want me to tell them about them. They are special stones to them and they think they may be saying something that they don't understand. They ask me to see what they are saying. That pile out there are stones that weren't saying anything." He sort of chuckled. I was silent waiting for more. He then picked up a palmful of stones that were on the table in front of us and told me about them. He said people brought them to him to interpret them. "I had them here for a long time and couldn't figure out what they meant. So, I threw them out on the pile. I had to go to town for supplies that day and when I got back and unlocked the door, they were back on the table. I'm still not sure what they are saying but I'm working on it."

What do we make of this? Do we have what others would call superstition here, or do we have a new understanding of the stones based on Spotted Horse's story that they were capable of things we had not believed before? Our modern society would scoff at stories like this. They would say they personally had never witnessed anything similar. They would brush off the story by saying "Stones don't do those things." And the medicine men and women might reply: "They don't do them for you!" But stones are part of our traditional experiences whether Christian or Native. Faith calls us to believe that we are capable of things that we had not believed before.

Dr. Thom White Wolf Fassett
Seneca
Retired Elder
Upper New York Conference

Questions for Discussion

1. Dr. Mann speaks very lovingly about the earth. How do you think of the earth and what does it mean to you?
2. If we are to stop the desecration of the earth, where do we need to start? What are actions you can take in this regard?
3. What do you think God expects of us in regard to being caretakers of the earth?
4. Have you ever had an experience of God through some aspect of the natural world? Briefly share your experience.

Chapter 10

Visions

One of the many reasons I am thankful for being Native American is because we are a people of visions. As indigenous people, our survival has depended on holding fast to visions that elevated our spirits to places beyond the suffering of the present moment. I believe visions have the power to take us into the past and to offer insight into the lives of our ancestors. These visions connect us with the source of power which allowed our people to survive a holocaust.

As indigenous people of this present age, we live in cities and small communities; we live in rural areas and tribal towns; and we live near and on reservations. I believe one of the gifts from visions for this present time is the offering of empathy for one another. Our visions for this day build connections between us so that we celebrate one another's victories and mourn one another's losses.

And finally, as indigenous people, thankful to have a future to look toward, we offer our imaginations to set free our visions for a good life, seven generations and beyond. Creator God offers us inspiration and hope, the positive foundations for visions into the future.

In our discussions on visions, Henri shared about the vision and prophecy of Sweet Medicine of the Cheyenne. Within my tribe, there are also persons known as prophets who shared their visions with the people. Our conversations reminded me of biblical prophecies which must be carefully considered, prayerfully approached and solemnly examined by thinking and feeling human beings to ascertain the prophecy's implications.

For folks who have not been exposed to Native American spirituality and ceremonial ways, the prophecies that Henri shares may seem unusual, however, the same may be said of the prophecies of the Book of Revelation, for example. I believe Henri is trusting us to listen and respect what is shared and I have no doubt she prayed to Creator God before she shared such intimate aspects of her faith. I, for one, am thankful for her faith and her sharing.

Visions Among Native Peoples

Native Americans accept and honor a person's ability to be guided by dreams, to have contact with the world of spirit, to experience a vision, or to see into the future. There have been some such visionaries throughout history who were blessed with this special ability. Black Elk of the Lakota and Wovoka of the Paiute are two such individuals. Another is Sweet Medicine, a prophet of the Cheyenne, who could see into the future and before they ever arrived in their lands, he told them about the "numerous, handsome, light-skinned strangers," who were coming, whose ways were different, even to their manner of dress that would make them look as if they were confined in sacks. He told them of the things they would bring that would change their ways of life and their form of education that would cause their children to lose their tribal identity.

Sweet Medicine, Prophet of the Cheyenne

Sweet Medicine was a special child, who possessed extraordinary abilities. When he reached adulthood, he was seemingly called north to the Cheyenne sacred mountain Bear Butte, located near current day Sturgis, South Dakota. He stayed within that mountain lodge for four years where he was taught by all the spirit powers of the world who assembled there to teach him.

Thus, he brought the Cheyenne tribal covenant and accompanying ceremony out of Bear Butte. Upon his return, he established their traditional government, the Council of Forty-four

Peace Chiefs, and the warrior societies, whose members are known as headsmen. Moreover, he established their tribal law ways which prohibited intra-tribal murder, and advised them to be honest, to never lie or cheat, to never marry relatives, and to maintain and defend the Cheyenne way of life. Additionally, he implored the people to always remember him and his teachings. With his power to see into the future, he prepared the people for that different time by instituting many good teachings, primary among them, peace. Sweet Medicine exerted a positive influence upon the Cheyenne, and his influence is still alive today.

After having lived with the Cheyenne four long lives of a person, Sweet Medicine sadly gave them his farewell prophecy, some of which were exceptionally ominous. Included among them is the prediction that a baby is to be born with a full set of teeth, who is to be a cannibal and devour everyone. Perhaps this baby is the symbol of society's rampant consumerism and economic greed which hold worldwide implications of disaster. There also is to be a young woman running down the road, howling like a wolf whose message will not be understood. Could this be a warning from the four-legged people, whom humans no longer understand? He also said that the people had to be aware of the weather, observing it from the windows and doors of their homes, and taking precautionary measures against any impending danger. Sweet Medicine then said the earth would burn, which could be global warming and climate change.

Human beings must listen with their hearts and minds to such prophecies and act responsibly as good relatives to the universal human family. They need to protect their Mother the Earth from continued natural resource extraction and contamination. People must decrease their human footprints, conserve energy, and think green. Native Americans have always cautioned each generation to walk lightly upon Earth. Because living gently on earth was good in the past, it also is good for the future. Thus, acting responsibly at the individual level holds great potential and promise for the world.

Dr. Henrietta Mann

Prophets are persons who open themselves to the voice of the Great Mystery and are willing to share this voice with the people.

They are not always persons who sit on mountain tops, many times they are the person sitting right next to us. Daphine Strickland is one of these persons. She experiences the voice of God in so many ways and strives to respond as a follower of Jesus Christ.

She is serving as a reserve lay delegate to the Southeastern Jurisdictional Conference later this year and has served the United Methodist Church in many ways, but one of her most visionary activities is found in her relationship with the young people in her church and community. Time and again I have witnessed Daphine bringing youth to United Methodist events, interacting with them, mentoring them. She is a woman who lives out of the vision and promise of her Creator. In her essay, she writes of the visionary life she has lived.

The Still Small Voice

Long before Columbus and other explorers arrived in the Americas, Native Americans have had visions. Many Natives accepted the arrival of their white brothers and sisters because of visions they had about white-skinned people coming to the Americas. This vision has been reported by several tribes from diverse parts of the country.

Crazy Horse, whose name might also be translated as Holy, Mystical or Inspired Horse, was a great warrior of the Oglala Lakota. He spent many days on vision quests which later helped him lead his people and acquire his name. At a young age he had many visions, one of which was to conceal his body by riding on one side of his horse. This contributed to his renown, as he was able to steal many horses from other tribes. Stealing horses in that day was more sport than what we consider stealing today. It was practiced among various tribes.

Visions Come in Many Forms

When I was young, visions came to me in the form of a still, small voice. I can see a vision in my mind or feel it in my heart.

Visions come in many forms—it may be a story to write and share, a picture to paint, or an idea for a piece of jewelry.

In the story of Samuel, found in 1 Samuel 3:1-11, the Bible says that when Samuel was a boy, God was speaking to him, but Samuel thought it was Eli, the priest who was teaching Samuel. Eli instructed Samuel to say "Speak Lord, for your servant is listening," in response to the voice that was calling Samuel's name. I, too, have always tried to listen when I have heard the voice of the Creator.

When I was 18 years old the Creator clearly spoke to me. I was told to go to church. I had two small girls and a husband. Though I loved them dearly, they were not enough to fill the deep void I felt living in the big city of Greensboro, North Carolina, apart from my Native people. My mother encouraged me to find a church there because she sensed that I needed more from life than caring for my family. As often as we could afford the gas, we went home to Robeson County in North Carolina, to be with our Native American community. It was 1964, and I always cried as we prepared to return to Greensboro, because we were leaving our Indian community to return to an urban, hostile environment in Greensboro. It was hostile because of the time in history, and because our skin was not the right shade.

One Saturday afternoon, a still small voice told me to go to church and I listened. That Sunday morning my daughters and I walked two blocks to Immanuel Baptist Church. This church was an all-white church in the fall of 1965, but they welcomed us with open arms and our lives changed forever. I accepted Jesus Christ as Savior and began my journey with Creator God. One year later my husband, Daniel, began going with us. In 1966 Immanuel Baptist Church, a Southern Baptist Church, took action to oppose the social norms of the Jim Crow South and opened its doors to all racial-ethnic people.

During this time, I recall seeing many visions long before they happened. In one vision I saw our plain church building outfitted with beautiful stained glass windows. To that point, all the stained glass I had ever seen tended to make church sanctuaries appear dark and foreboding, so my opinion of stained glass was not positive. Later, I served on the Building & Grounds Committee which made the decision to install stained glass windows in the church. When the work was complete we had the most beautiful stained glass windows in Greensboro. My vision had come true.

A Vision for Her Life

In 1989 I began working with a group of Native community leaders and Methodist leaders in Greensboro to provide a church where Native people would feel at home. There were many unchurched Native people in the area. Once we formed the Triad Native American United Methodist Church and received a pastor, my husband and one of my daughters committed themselves to serve the new congregation. My plan was to remain at Immanuel Baptist Church, but the Creator spoke to me and said, "I am the God of the Baptists and of the Methodists and you will go where I send you." I have been at Triad ever since.

While in college years later, I wrote a paper on storytelling and a voice spoke to me clearly saying, "You are a storyteller. You are to keep your peoples' stories alive and remember that storytellers are the historians, the psychologists and the keepers of traditions among your people." Wow! This came to me when I was at a very low point of my life. My vision of not being hopeless, but blessed by the Creator carried me through.

Later, I was asked to give a blessing at the college I was attending for their commencement service. I gathered cedar for the smudging and a vision came to me of a large bag of sage that my tribes, the Lumbee and Tuscarora, used for seasoning. My sister had given it to me before she died. I had a vision that I was to use this sage for smudging. I did a blessing for that commencement service; and again, when I graduated in 1999. Praise God.

Today I am a better listener and a visionary because I feel more in spirit with the Creator. I carry along paper and when I have a vision I write it down. Sometimes the vision is in the form of words of comfort for a friend, an idea for a grant, a story, and at other times it might foretell a death. Visions are of great importance to Native peoples because they are sent by the Creator.

Daphine Locklear Strickland
Lumbee-Tuscarora
Triad Native American United Methodist Church
Western North Carolina Conference

Questions for Discussion

1. Share with one another a vision you have had that connected you with the past, present and/or future.
2. In reading about the life and visions of the prophet, Sweet Medicine, how do his life and visions compare with prophets with whom you are familiar from the Bible?
3. How have you reacted responsibly when you have heard a Native American and/or biblical prophecy? Have you shared about this prophecy with others in your family or community?
4. Daphine Strickland writes about visions coming in many forms. What are some of the ways you have experienced a vision from the Creator within your own life?

Chapter 11

Indigenous Peoples: of Confession, Repentance and Forgiveness

At the 2008 General Conference, the decision was made that at the 2012 General Conference the whole church would engage in an Act of Repentance on "Healing relationships with indigenous persons." In this essay, the author approaches the topic from the perspective of his indigenous roots and identity.

Hold a moment longer! Not quite yet, gentlemen! Before you go I would like to say just a word about the Philippine business. I have been criticized a good deal about the Philippines, but don't deserve it. The truth is I didn't want the Philippines, and when they came to us, as a gift from the gods, I did not know what to do with them. When the Spanish War broke out Dewey was at Hongkong, and I ordered him to go to Manila and to capture or destroy the Spanish fleet, and he had to; because, if defeated, he had no place to refit on that side of the globe, and if the Dons were victorious they would likely cross the Pacific and ravage our Oregon and California coasts. And so he had to destroy the Spanish fleet, and did it! But that was as far as I thought then.

When I next realized that the Philippines had dropped into our

*laps I confess I did not know what to do with them. I sought counsel
from all sides—Democrats as well as Republicans—but got little
help. I thought first we would take only Manila; then Luzon; then
other islands perhaps also. I walked the floor of the White House
night after night until midnight; and I am not ashamed to tell you,
gentlemen, that I went down on my knees and prayed Almighty God
for light and guidance more than one night. And one night late it
came to me this way—I don't know how it was, but it came: (1) That
we could not give them back to Spain—that would be cowardly and
dishonorable; (2) that we could not turn them over to France and
Germany—our commercial rivals in the Orient—that would be
bad business and discreditable; (3) that we could not leave them to
themselves—they were unfit for self-government—and they would
soon have anarchy and misrule over there worse than Spain's was;
and (4) that there was nothing left for us to do but to take them all,
and to educate the Filipinos, and uplift and civilize and Christianize
them, and by God's grace do the very best we could by them, as our
fellow-men for whom Christ also died. And then I went to bed, and
went to sleep, and slept soundly, and the next morning I sent for the
chief engineer of the War Department (our map-maker), and I told
him to put the Philippines on the map of the United States (pointing
to a large map on the wall of his office), and there they are, and
there they will stay while I am President!*

(Source: General James Rusling, "Interview with President William
McKinley," *The Christian Advocate* 22 January 1903, 17. The
interview recounts a meeting on November 21, 1899 between
Pres. McKinley and a delegation of five clergymen representing
the General Missionary Committee of the [Northern] Methodist
Episcopal Church. Courtesy of General Commission on Archives
and History of The United Methodist Church, Madison, New Jersey.)

Rootedness and Anchor

It is appropriate that I begin my essay by sharing the words of
President William McKinley from the year 1899. For my homeland,
the Philippines, this year became the advent of what had come to be
called, "Manifest Destiny." Manifest Destiny was the philosophical

90

and political approach of the United States toward the indigenous peoples of the world. In President McKinley's statement, you can clearly hear the articulation that the conquest and destruction of the indigenous ways of the peoples of Philippines had been revealed to him by God, therefore making whatever actions necessary to accomplish this end acceptable.

I started writing about my indigenous roots as a matter of claiming self and identity that was submerged for years. My claim to my indigenous roots was an act of anchoring myself in both the land of my birth and the many lands in which I have been privileged to meet many other peoples and cultures. This includes the United States where I now reside.

My encounters of peoples and cultures different from mine made me appreciate their claims of self and identity. These encounters, for the most part, enriched my knowledge of other peoples and cultures even as it led me to both question and challenge mine. And all for the better, I must say.

I found security in the knowledge that others knew and appreciated me because I, too, appreciated them. Over the years I have learned that there is no greater security than that which is secured by mutual respect. Respect rooted in conquest is not true respect; it thrives on the back of exploitation. This is why the "discovery" and colonization of indigenous peoples is a matter to be taken seriously. Following European colonialism and conquest, and the introduction of slavery which further exploited and oppressed peoples; their territories and resources were ravaged; and indigenous cultures corrupted.

The manner in which Western religions were introduced— through the violence of sword and the cross for fifteenth-century colonial powers like Spain and Portugal, and through the rifle and the Bible for nineteenth-century colonial power like the United States—demeans the love that Jesus Christ offered so freely.

(Re)Covering Self and Identity

My father was a storyteller of great skill. He was known in our town as someone who could enliven public gatherings with the wit and wisdom that came with the stories and anecdotes he told and retold. He had a public identity that I eventually took on. After all, I was his adoring son who went around the social and public gatherings to learn and eventually partake of his gift of storytelling. As I increasingly studied the English language and learned more of Western culture, I found, to my dismay, that I began to lose the indigenous gift of storytelling.

My father earned the respect of other people by nurturing honest dealings and loving and transparent relationships. He was born poor and remained poor until he died at age 86. But his poverty was characterized with integrity. He may have been impoverished of earthly goods but he had an abundance of goodwill and honor. He was the epitome of perseverance. Learning his discipline and character worked well for me in the years of my youth on to adulthood, especially as I grew into my own person, found my indigenous roots, and anchored myself with the values of the land of my birth.

My father was a public man even as my mother was the opposite. She was very reserved publicly but very lively and sociable among family and friends. She and my father were equally loved for the stories they told us. Storytelling was the vehicle through which their experience led to family tradition. They could read and write, but the oral transmission of knowledge through stories that were full of wisdom and blessing was what helped shape and mold my character. Who I am today—the core of my identity and moral being—are rooted in the stories, myths, fables and all.

Indigenous knowledge depends on a great deal of storytelling. It is one method that is now both at risk and preserved by technological advances. Oral tradition is being eroded as a method of communication by new media and digital technologies, while by the same media, storytelling can also be preserved for posterity.

It was not until my adult life that I discovered a layer of self and identity crucial to my being, knowing and doing as the person I am. I have not until adulthood acknowledged and claimed it publicly and openly. My mother comes from a family of Ibanag heritage. Ibanag is one of several ethnolinguistic and indigenous groups in the Philippines.

When I was a young boy and later in high school, was I ashamed of my indigenous heritage? Not really. But I did not know the significance of that part of my identity until I became an adult. In fact, even my mother was not as keen as I am now in claiming a stake of that heritage.

(Re)Naming the Powers

From hindsight, I now know that survival is a vital motivator in the search for self and identity. Across the centuries to the present day, indigenous peoples have been struggling to assert their right to self-determination. That struggle rises up in the face of efforts to marginalize, minoritize and even cut them off from the umbilical cord that connects them to Mother Earth.

My father was Ilocano, a linguistic grouping in the Philippines that assimilated quickly into the ways and culture of the conquering Spanish conquistadores. Close to 400 years of Spanish conquest and a hundred years of U.S. imperial conquest in the Philippines has resulted in the complete oppression of a people whose indigenous ways of governance were eventually replaced by something foreign to their indigenous practice. The legal system in the Philippines even today is largely Spanish and American, requiring every student of Philippine law to be equally familiar with these two foreign legal regimes.

Nationhood and nation-building remain a continuing challenge for the Philippines and to Filipinos, not the least Philippine indigenous peoples. Until my country's own indigenous roots are allowed to sprout in order that native ways of governance and development may contribute to nation-building, especially in the areas of economy and culture, it may yet continue to be molded in an alien culture, a culture whose inner identity and outer appearance have nothing to do with who the Filipino people really are—their native Filipino loob—of soul and spirit.

Through the might of Western sword and cross, and the forced imposition of mystifying Latin rites and rituals from the Catholic Church, the indigenous ways of knowing and doing that have existed for many centuries were devalued, judged as backward and unfit, hence bound for elimination. Through rifle and Bible, conquest has introduced a violent rather than a loving and a forgiving God. In considering repentance for those who played a part in the conquest and oppression of indigenous peoples of the Philippines or indigenous peoples anywhere in the world, an act of repentance must fully acknowledge this forced loss of indigenous memories. It must rewrite what has been eliminated from historical records: that

93

in winning their souls for Christ, many indigenous nations have been victims of acts that are of genocidal proportions.

Any and all acts of healing that recover the wholeness of indigenous peoples must address the ruptures in history that have violently submerged memories and remembrances, even lives and livelihoods. Repentance, forgiveness and healing must necessarily restore the right relationships that will reinstate both indigenous and non-indigenous peoples as equal members of humanity.

(Re)Covering Sacred Ground and Space

To (re)tell my story in first person, and dare consider it alongside the struggles of my sister and brother indigenous peoples is an exercise in recovering memory. And it is humbling.

To claim wholeness for myself is to also lay claim to the wholeness of every indigenous person, including my mother and her Ibanag family. This claim, I pray, will heal at least for me, the losses in my historical and biological memory. Indigenous peoples, as all peoples, are connected to a web of relationships that tangle and mingle us with the rest of the universe. We are each related to the entirety of God's creation. We are brothers and sisters in Christ. That makes us sacred beings and the ground on which we stand and the horizon that gives us the vista of God's spacious creation are equally sacred. There is no true spirituality that severs one divine creation from another. Every strand supports the creative web.

To claim my identity, and that of my mother, is a claim on self-discovery. I claim my wholeness as intended by my Creator. By claiming my indigenous identity, I also claim my existence, even my dreams, which are equally inhabited by indigenous signs and symbols that also have claims on my spirituality.

This claim is my own way of challenging and defying a long-standing and centuries-old doctrine that discovered, or so it claimed, the indigenous peoples of the world, their identities, territories, resources and all. This so-called "doctrine of discovery" has resulted in the destruction of indigenous cultures. It meant the defeat and conquest of a people whose resources were then claimed on behalf of the crown heads of the Europe.

(Re)Location and Claiming Space

Many thousands of miles away, in the Philippines, where my mother's family is settled, learning about the Ibanags is even more challenging now that I reside in the United States. My consolation is that I work in a setting where I can learn of the plight of indigenous peoples around the world and give focus to promoting indigenous people's human rights.

I write in the first person as my way of recovering the hidden indigenous person in me. It is to claim space and equality for who God made me. I make this claim not in spite of my being indigenous, but because I am indigenous.

Up until my adult life, I introduced myself only as an Ilocano and have repressed the identity owed from my mother. I speak fluent Ilocano but only know a little of Ibanag, except for two songs that my mother taught me in full.

I went to school from elementary all the way to college perfecting the colonial language of English which was brought by Americans to the Philippines. I learned both written and spoken English the hard way. For every word in the Ilocano language that I used, I was fined five cents. This all happened at Thoburn Memorial Academy, the United Methodist high school which I attended. The fine was a punishment for speaking my mother tongue and an incentive to learn the colonial language, which was the official language of education, commerce and trade.

I did learn enough English to make me feel I had an edge in life and living compared to those who did not take English seriously for reasons I am sure are as valid as my own intentions. As my use of the English language increased, I felt the power of the oppression grip my thinking and imagination.

Today, I am increasingly thinking and analyzing in ways and forms that respect my indigenous roots. I make a point to include ongoing scholarly research on and by indigenous peoples. I am intentionally attending events led by indigenous peoples so that I can learn more of who we are as peoples.

An Act of Repentance Requires Forgiveness; Forgiveness Requires Confession

Imagining a world where we have come to terms with our confession of responsibility, acts of repentance, and search for forgiveness, involves restoring indigenous peoples to the world of humanity where they are free to determine their own destinies and live in relationship with other ethnicities, large and small.

To seek forgiveness in our act of repentance seems to necessitate confessing our responsibility in the oppression and destruction of indigenous peoples, rendering them alienated from their own culture and of other cultures. Alienation and marginalization saps positive energies and corrupts the spirituality that comes out of it—for both the alienator and alienated.

Marginalization and minoritization consigns indigenous peoples to inferiority and prevents them from meaningful interaction in almost every human endeavor, including political and economic which are activities that have defined so much their lives but has excluded them from participation.

To illustrate, in my homeland marginalization has pushed indigenous peoples from places where the dominant culture inhabited, mostly into the mountains. Restoration will now involve the recovery of lost territory as well as the assertion of peoplehood so that indigenous peoples interact with society as people of dignity and pride.

What Repentance Requires and Forgiveness Demands

Indigenous peoples see themselves from the very beginning in the totality of the cosmos in which they are but one critical component. It is in this light that they too have participated in standards setting, in the context of the United Nations and other international gatherings, as important.

Indigenous peoples participate in standard-setting perhaps as an anticipatory act. Through participation, there is anticipation of a better, more friendly, and more peaceful, more just, more sustainable world. And one that is hospitable to original peoples, native peoples, first peoples, and indigenous peoples. Indigenous peoples have realized that if they do not participate, the standard setting process will go on. If this process goes on without them, the worst for them could continue.

Through almost a century of representation, and at least three decades of negotiation, the Universal Declaration of the Rights of Indigenous Peoples is a reality today. But one that is born out of struggle and not from a silver platter.

The presence of indigenous peoples in the halls of multi-nation negotiation remains low. Even then, their presence in decision making – in what happens in their territories and domains and at various local, national, regional and international settings – is increasingly acknowledged as crucial. The historic approval in 2000, by the United Nations Economic and Social Council, of the Permanent Forum on Indigenous Issues is a signal example of this crucial role.

Among indigenous peoples, it is quite well known that as early as 1923, Chief Deskaheh of the Haudenosaunee Nation in the U.S. travelled to Geneva, Switzerland to present to the League of Nations a defense of the rights of his people to live under their own laws, in their own land, and under their own faith. He returned home in 1925, not having been allowed to speak. His vision, however, inspired many generations of indigenous peoples after him.

A similar journey was done by Maori religious leader T. W. Ratana. He travelled first to London seeking an audience with King George to protest the breaking of the Treaty of Waitangi concluded between his people, the Maori, and New Zealand (Aotearoa). The treaty gave the Maoris ownership of their lands. Not granted access to King George, Ratana sent part of his delegation to Geneva at the League of Nations. He joined them there in 1925, but still, denied access. His actions, too, have inspired those who came after.

An honest to goodness act of repentance allows for indigenous peoples to name and articulate the harm done to them. It is truth-telling from their perspective. It includes naming the historic injustices that have hurt and marginalized a people. Writing one's narrative is itself a painful act for indigenous peoples, as I can now testify.

Indigenous People's Spirituality: What Apology and Confession Exacts

Spirituality pervades the entire being, knowing and doing of indigenous peoples. Their spirituality is in their struggles, and in their struggles is spirituality. When they assert their stewardship of land, indigenous peoples are also asserting their spirituality. Rev. Gelung Gondarra, an Australian Aborigine, expressed it best this way:

Our people are called nature farmers. We get and give back to the land. We know that the land becomes like our mother. The Mother Earth produces life for the people to enjoy, and provides shelter and protection, and holds the values for our people's survival. The land gives us identity of who we are. It gives us knowledge to build strong relationships, which bind us together into a solid bond, which nobody can destroy.

Indigenous peoples reverence for the entire cosmos–the Mother Earth, the Pacha Mama–and their struggles to ensure and exact this reverence, is spirituality of an order that have far too long been denied, ignored, denigrated, even demolished and dismantled by many dominant religions, especially those that have been instrumental in their colonization.

An act of repentance must proceed from a prior act – a statement of responsibility in the marginalization and oppression of indigenous peoples. Repentance without confession would be hollow, much like cheap grace.

Under the so-called Doctrine of Discovery, indigenous peoples were not human beings. In U.S. President William McKinley's claim on the Philippine Islands, the Christian claim to not just politically claim the Philippines but to also claim it for Christ is so telling in what he said: "there was nothing left for us to do but to take them all, and to educate the Filipinos, and uplift and civilize and Christianize them, and by God's grace do the very best we could by them, as our fellow-men for whom Christ also died."

Apology and confession is constitutive of a genuine and honest act of repentance. Beyond acknowledgment of responsibility and complicity, such acts must name the historic and contemporary forms of harm done on both indigenous peoples and non-indigenous.

Historic slavery and colonialism, and its ongoing manifestations, including unbridled globalization, spell human rights violation on indigenous peoples. The continuing disregard for the principle of "free, prior and informed consent" is one such egregious violation on the self-determination that indigenous peoples assert.

The Pursuit of Wholeness: Finding Ways to Heal

As the 2012 General Conference of The United Methodist Church (April 23-May 4, 2012, Tampa, Florida, USA) prepares the church for an "Act of Repentance," it is surely wise to ask ourselves, individually and collectively, "Repentance from what and forgiveness by whom?"

It is worth repeating here what is often said but almost always hard to follow: "No reconciliation without forgiveness; no forgiveness without repentance; and no repentance without restitution."

How do we indeed move from confession to repentance so that our act is credible and acceptable? What forms of redress and restitution will truly express repentance that might move into reconciliation and forgiveness?

It seems to me that reconciliation is attitudinal ("I will not steal your land anymore.") while rectification is behavioral ("I will return the land that I stole.")

Among indigenous peoples attitude and behavior must join up so that the search for wholeness is truly holistic—for indigenous peoples and everyone, including the diversity and plurality of the cosmos that is God's creation. The joining up can be expressed in respecting and following the principle of "free, prior and informed consent."

This principle gives to a community and its peoples the right to give or withhold its consent to proposed projects that may affect the lands they customarily own, occupy or otherwise use. This principle is crucial, for example, in the struggle of indigenous peoples to prohibit unsustainable mining practices in their ancestral domains and territories.

The Act of Repentance and the Anticipation of Forgiveness

It took and is taking centuries to move from truth telling to apology and confession, and then on to an act of repentance. It may also take that long for the repentance to be received and move into forgiveness by the peoples and communities that were hurt.

We must be realistic about the possibilities that an act of repentance offers even as we must joyfully anticipate what forgiveness might open up for the embrace of peoples once hurt by another. This is no less than that same search for peace and pursuing it so that the peace of Christ that passes all understanding pervades every and all relationships.

To anticipate forgiveness is to imagine reconciliation, reconstruction and reconstitution in ways we may not have seen or experienced before. An act of repentance must not be denied by the possibilities such an act brings to mind. It must move forward with the vision of how God might yet surprise God's people and cause us to praise and sing "in awesome wonder."

This paper expands an article that was originally published in Church and Society, a journal of The Presbyterian Church of the USA

Rev. Liberato C. Bautista
Assistant General Secretary for
United Nations and International
Affairs of the General Board of
Church and Society of The United
Methodist Church.
Ordained Deacon
Northern Philippines Annual
Conference of the Philippines
Central Conference

Questions for Discussion

1. Liberato Bautista writes about the journey of discovering his indigenous roots. How important are your indigenous roots? What role does your Native identity play in your Christian life?

2. The author writes "in winning their souls for Christ, many indigenous nations have been victims of acts that are of genocidal proportions." How are you able to make sense of this historical paradox as a follower of Jesus Christ ?

3. In considering how the UMC can participate in an act of repentance for the harm done to Native and indigenous peoples, confession must come first. What do you feel the UMC needs to confess in regard to indigenous peoples?

4. A major part of the author's journey was rediscovering the gifts of his parents and how they contributed to shaping the person he is. What part did your parents, grandparents or other relations play in shaping who you are?

Chapter 12

Repentance

At the 2008 General Conference, the decision was made that at the 2012 General Conference the whole church would engage in an Act of Repentance on "Healing relationships with indigenous persons."

The topic of repentance is approached as a letter to brothers and sisters who form the body of The Church.

A Letter to the Church of Jesus Christ

Again, the kingdom of heaven is like a merchant in search of fine pearls; on finding one pearl of great value, he went and sold all that he had and bought it. (Matthew 13:45-46)

You offered us a pearl wrapped in an iron shell and we broke our teeth upon it.

Dear Beloved Church,

I write this letter to you on a cold winter day in the year 2012. To have this opportunity to speak directly with you in this way is beyond my wildest imagining. You have been described as the body of Christ (1 Corinthians 12) with each of us serving as parts of the body. Together, we are the hands, feet and voice of Jesus Christ in this world. As I write this letter, I do so knowing that I am part of you — one tiny interlocked piece of the puzzle that you are.

You are the sacred entity through which the Holy Spirit walks its path in this world. We, who are disciples of Jesus Christ, find our life and identity through you. We experience our greatest joy and comfort for our deepest sorrow through you, our Church.

I also know you as the imperfect, self-centered and exclusionary organization created from our human strivings. You are the human church who strayed from the true message of Jesus Christ and forced upon many nations of the world a false vision of what it means to be a Christian disciple. By forcing us to abandon our identity as children of a loving Creator, fearfully and wonderfully made, in order to become what we were not—European clones—we entered what would become for many of us a spiral of death rather than a circle of life.

Countless Voices

As I write, I am aware that my voice is a representative voice, standing in the stead for uncounted masses of souls. These are the souls of Native and indigenous peoples from across the world.

These souls cry out from a past that dates from first contact with the strangers who came from faraway places and brought good news along with enslavement, destruction and genocide.

These souls cry out from the present time. Wishing, hoping, praying that the Church to which they are called will seize this moment and engage in true repentance.

These souls cry out from the future. Generations yet unborn—far beyond even seven generations—will they believe that the Church of Jesus Christ includes them?

Walking in Balance

A critical concept for indigenous people all around the world is the idea of walking in balance. This is the way that the Creator calls us to make our journey of life. We walk in a sense of balance with all that surrounds us and all of which we are a part. I believe that the notions of repentance, healing and reconciliation find their fullness within this concept of balance. When I strive to live in right relationship with all that surrounds me, this is a call for me to be accountable to my brothers and my sisters—to all of the human beings in the world, to all of the animal and plant beings, to mother earth herself and ultimately to Creator God.

Repentance as a Process

For Christians, repentance is a cornerstone of our faith. The foundation of Jesus' message was to repent and recognize the reign of God had come near. As human beings, we often take the easy road by viewing repentance as a one dimensional experience. It is as if that moment of repenting happens as a singular event in our lives, an isolated experience that becomes self-justifying to us—by recognizing our need to repent, we win the prize—forgiveness.

What I believe is that repentance is a process that engages us in several connected actions of heart, of mind, and of spirit. I believe that the journey of repentance begins at the same place that it ends—in *relationship*. It begins when we find ourselves in *relationships* with other parts of the world, with other people and other parts of creation, and with the institutions of the world; and we subsequently make the decision to open ourselves to examination of these *relationships*. It ends when we find ourselves in continued *relationship* with all of these entities and we understand that the quality of our own existence can only be measured in the context of our shared life together. We are accountable to God through these *relationships*.

The Invisible Ones

As a Native American I am intimately aware that one of the greatest burdens born by Native people in the Americas and by indigenous peoples around the world, is that we have become the invisible ones. Because of the history of this country, we are considered a people who have been conquered, who now, in essence, belong to the dominant ones in our nation. We are no longer people who have a significance in this present day and time. We are thought of as relics or figures from the past who have no contribution to make toward the future. Many of our non-Native friends, who are our brothers and sisters in Christ, will read these words and say, "Not so, this is not true, we know that you are here, we remember you." However I must compel you to listen to us and hear our cry which comes from living within the flesh that God has given us.

Are you willing to embark on this process of repentance by being in *relationship* with us?

I offer to you, beloved Church, four steps that I believe are essential for repentance.

First Step: Can you see us?

When I consider the steps that are essential for a journey through repentance, healing and eventual arrival at reconciliation, I believe the first step is to simply become *aware* of that person, of that cause, of that entity that has been wronged. This is a first and essential step for our Church, our United Methodist Mother Church. It must be acknowledged publicly and with firmness and conviction that,

Yes, Native American people and Native indigenous people around the world, we recognize you, we see you there and we are willing to hear your story now. We are willing to know the road you have walked. We acknowledge you, and we are ready to receive what you have to say. As your Church, the body of Jesus Christ, we are here for you.

The act of repentance is first, that action of turning away from the things that hurt others, that are harmful to our world, our Church and our family of life upon this earth; and second, the act of repentance means doing a new thing. Before we can turn toward a new possibility and do a new thing, we must first re-orient ourselves to see and acknowledge all of the other beings connected to us through the web of life.

My brothers and sisters of Christ's Church, we must first acknowledge that human beings who are different from us are also a part of our world. As a first step toward repentance and reconciliation it is vital to simply know, accept and respect that native and indigenous peoples are here and we have been here for the eternity of God's Creation. We have worshipped God for as long as we have walked the earth.

Can you see us?

As I recall going through the process of formal education from elementary school to graduate school and seminary, I have the recollection of being an invisible student. Paradoxically, the way I figured out I was invisible was through my teachers' responses to me. There were many times when I surprised my teachers with the high quality of my work and I would hear the question, "Did *you* really do this?" or "Is this *your* work?" I imagined the teachers who said such things to me rarely saw me sitting quietly in their classroom, although I seldom missed a day of school. Fortunately, there were just enough teachers who saw me and did not respond with surprise every time I did something right. They let me know they considered me a part of their world. I give thanks to Creator God for them.

Second Step: Can you hear us?

Throughout my career as both a social worker and a minister I have often worked with children. When with a sizable group of children I would often "tune them out." I am sure those of you who have found themselves in a group of children at your church or at home with your family have done this also. Sometimes in order to accomplish what I needed to get done, the chirping voices and multiple conversations would become a buzzing blur in my ears. There were also times, however, when I realized one of these voices needed my total attention. I am reminded of a time when I pastored a church with many children. Most of the children came from poor homes without transportation and I would pick them up in my car for children's ministry. As I drove along I would usually be thinking about what I needed to do for that evening's activity or something from my own life. One evening as I drove a noisy group of children to the church I tuned in to their several conversations for a brief moment. In that moment I heard the words "mom" and "jail." I gave over my full attention and learned that one child's mother was in jail. I could hear the sorrow in her voice. I made special time for that child who needed to tell her story. She needed to know that the Church where she came to worship God heard her voice and cared.

We have a story. We have many stories.

Our story is simply another facet of our shared walk upon the earth. To hear our story requires the deliberate step of suspending one's own story which is perpetually ringing in the ears. As we human beings walk and talk and live our lives, we are continually evaluating, comparing, amending and listening to our own story. The mechanism that processes feedback inside ourselves must come under our conscious control. It becomes an act of will to stop listening to one's own story and begin listening to someone else's.

There are a series of doors inside each of us. Psychologists call these defense mechanisms. They form boundaries within us through which only certain information is allowed to pass. We carefully guard the deepest parts of who we are by keeping the doors closed that would let in voices that challenge or threaten how we define ourselves. We are calling out to you, brothers and sisters of our Church, open those innermost doors of your hearts and let our voices enter.

Can you hear us?

<u>Third Step: Can you find Christ in us?</u>

And now, there is a third step that I commend to you as part of the circle that can lead from repentance to reconciliation. The third step is—after you see me, after you hear me—can you find Christ in me? This is an essential part of our life in Christ, that we are able to see Christ in one another. It is the great equalizer that Creator God has made available to us. Before repentance is possible we must see the face of the sacred in one another. So I ask you, when you look at me what do you see? Do you see a Native American woman of brown skin and dark hair whose life and purpose relate only to the past? Does my voice come to you from the margins that are only periodically to be listened to? If you see Native Americans and indigenous peoples as irrelevant to the life of United Methodism, you are not ready for repentance.

Mother Teresa has long been a hero of mine. I recall hearing her speak about the work done in places like Calcutta where she led a group of nuns who served the sick and dying. She spoke of the beginning of her ministry. She was on her way to a teaching assignment. At that time in her life her assignment was to teach in a Christian school. She was walking through the poorest part of the city and as she took a side step to go around a man lying in the street, he looked up at her and their eyes met. In that sacred moment she saw Christ in the face of that dying man. She knew her path was meant to include this man and the Christ she had found in his eyes.

Can you find Christ in your Native American brothers and sisters? Can you find Christ in the indigenous peoples of color throughout the world?

Fourth Step: Will you claim us?

The final step I would share with you flows from the concept of being related to all living beings on the earth. To be related to someone, you *claim* them as your kin. They are part of your family. You are in relationship with them and connected to them. When you are connected to one another (imagine a spider web), then movement in the smallest part of the connection impacts every other part of the connection. Through this connection you feel the pain, suffering, hope and joy of all your relatives. In its very best application, this is how our United Methodist connection operates. Churches within our faith communion choose to be *in community* with one another. This connection is an essential element of our theology and polity. As Jesus Christ claims each of us, we are called to claim one another.

On Being Native American

One of the greatest blessings in my life is being Native American. I have travelled to many places throughout the U.S. and have been among many different Native nations. No matter the place or the tribe, I can count on my Native American relatives to claim me, even if I have never before met these relatives. We share warm words, talk about our tribes and who we know. We extend to one another a mutual sense of sanctuary and safety within each other's presence. Most of the time I am invited to someone's home for a meal or offered a bed for the night. I am welcomed as family.

Native American people have some of the most challenging demographics with which to live. In the U.S. we are at the bottom of the economic ladder, we have high dropout rates for our youth, high unemployment rates and high rates of incarceration. Our people suffer extreme levels of alcohol and drug addiction and have among the highest rates in the world for suicide of young people.

So why am I so blessed by being Native American?

It is because I am *claimed* by my Native American people. I am deeply embedded within a web of humanity that connects me to others who *claim* me as their relative; and I walk upon the earth with a sense of knowing who I am in a wholistic sense. The connection with my community reinforces the love of God in my life.

So, beloved Church, are you ready to claim us, the Native and indigenous peoples of the world?

In closing this letter, I confess that I have also been guilty of exclusion in my own thinking. Perhaps sharing a part of my own spiritual journey will be helpful to you as you consider the upcoming Acts of Repentance.

My Confession

Many moons ago I served as pastor to a Native American congregation. The church building where this congregation worshipped was a wood frame structure nearly fifty years old. It had been repaired many times over the years and had reached the point where it could no longer simply be repaired. It needed to be replaced. The congregation made the decision to work together to build a new church building. We knew it would take time to bring this dream to reality. There were some families in the church with decent jobs, but many more lived on fixed incomes or held minimum wage jobs and struggled to make ends meet. Our church applied and was accepted to be a "Volunteers in Mission" project within our conference. This meant that volunteer teams from our sister United Methodist churches from across the U.S. would be directed to help with the labor needed to build our new church.

I was informed by the VIM office that a retired architect from a very large church in a nearby city might be willing to help us with our project. I needed to meet with him and share our vision, and hopefully, engage his interest. I found myself surprised that such an educated and wealthy individual might possibly be drawn to our project.

Growing up in a poor family, my path had rarely crossed with those who lived in wealth. Additionally, my world revolved around the Native American community. I spent most of my days with little or no contact with persons from other racial-ethnic backgrounds. In looking back, I can see that I felt separated from my Christian brother, the architect, by virtue of him being a wealthy white man.

After our initial meeting, not only did he become interested in our building project, he entered into *relationship* with all of us at our little Native American church. He heard our story. He saw beauty in our children. He found wisdom in our elders. He saw Christ in us.

In addition to sharing his architectural gifts with us, this man brought enlightenment to me as a human being. He violated my expectations in a good way by being one of the most generous persons I have been privileged to know. He was certainly generous in sharing his time and talents, but he was also generous in sharing his very self. He helped to answer what was for me a troubling question asked in the 10th chapter of the book of Mark.

When it is more difficult for the wealthy to get into God's Kingdom than it is for a camel to go through the eye of a needle, how do the wealthy get into the Kingdom of God?

Well, I know it happens. I know a wealthy man who will be at the banquet table in the Kingdom of God. Through my relationship with him, I was led to repent.

I hope some of what I have shared might be helpful to you, dear Church, as you consider what it means to repent. This letter, started many weeks ago when a cold wind was blowing, is now finished as early spring warmth is bringing forth many of my green garden friends.

I look through my window, thinking of you in faraway places and I wish you God's blessing.

In Christ,

Anita Phillips

Questions for Discussion

1. How do you experience the worldwide Church of Jesus Christ? What are your thoughts when you contemplate being part of a universal Church that includes people very different from you, maybe even people who disregard or disrespect you?
2. How have you experienced repentance and forgiveness in your Christian walk?
3. Do you think it is possible for the entire United Methodist Church to repent? Why or why not?
4. Do you feel it is important for the United Methodist Church to repent of wrongs against Native American and indigenous peoples of the world? Why or why not?
5. What are examples of wrongs done by the Church against native and indigenous people in your nation?
6. If there was repentance and healing related to these wrongs, what would the results look like?

Additional Resources

This is a very short bibliography which includes only the most fundamental of readings. There are vast resources which offer in-depth study of Native American culture, spirituality and history, as well as bodies of work within many academic disciplines such as education, sociology and psychology. We encourage readers to explore these resources.

Bigelow, Bill, Peterson, Bob.(eds.). *Rethinking Columbus* (2nd Edition). Milwaukee: Rethinking Schools Press, 1998.

Buckley, Ray. *Dancing with a Brave Spirit – Telling the Truth About Native America (Revised). Nashville: UMCOM, 2005-2008.*

Deloria, Jr., Vine. *God is Red* (2nd Edition). Golden, Colorado: Fulcrum Publishing, 1992.

Fassett, Thom White Wolf. *Giving Our Hearts Away – Native American Survival.* New York: Women's Division, General Board of Global Ministries, The United Methodist Church, 2008.

Kidwell, Clara Sue, Homer Noley, George E. Tinker. *A Native American Theology.* New York: Orbis Books, 2001.

Momaday, N. Scott. *House Made of Dawn.* New York: Harper, 1968.

Neihardt, John G. *Black Elk Speaks* (8th Printing). New York: Pocket Books, 1975.

Noley, Homer. *First White Frost: Native Americans and United Methodism.* Nashville: Abingdon, 1991.

Tinker, George. *Missionary Conquest: The Gospel and Native American Cultural Genocide.* Minneapolis: Fortress Press, 1993.

Weaver, Jace (ed.). *Defending Mother Earth: Native American Perspectives on Environmental Justice*. New York: Orbis Books, 1996.

DVDs

500 Nations, PBS, 2004

Stories from the Circle of Life, Women's Division, GBGM, 2008

Native American Newspapers

www.nativetimes.com
www.indiancountrynews.com

Or you can enter "Native American" and "Newspapers" in your address bar and an extended list will be available.

Advance Projects

As a part of the follow up to the Acts of Repentance, churches and conferences of The United Methodist Church will be seeking ways to take action in the spirit of repentance. One way to take meaningful action is to support Native American and indigenous Advance Projects. The following brief list contains Native American projects of the Advance. To find projects serving indigenous peoples throughout the world, go to new.gbgm-umc.org/advance/projects/.

1. **Alaska Ethnic and Rural Camping and Conference Fund**
   931024 - North America, United States, Alaska, Anchorage
   Flying Native American and Eskimo children to Christian camps
   for church and   spiritual activities.

2. **Blackfeet United Methodist Parish**
   910092 - North America, United States, Montana, Browning
   To support continuing cultural, educational, healthcare services
   and outreach, and adding children's programs

3. **Cherokee United Methodist Ministry**
   731144 - North America, United States, North Carolina, Cherokee
   Developing programs that celebrate culture and bridge Christian
   faith with Cherokee spirituality

4. **Clinton Indian Church and Community Center**
   3020757 - North America, United States, Oklahoma
   Working to empower Native children and young people to dream
   of a future with hope

5. **Covenant Education Center**
   581262 - North America, United States, New Mexico, Shiprock
   Providing Christian day care and after school services for the
   Navajo community of Shiprock, NM

6. **Every Member in Ministry**
   791001 - North America, United States, North Carolina
   Sharing resources with 13 Native American congregations for
   programming, evangelism, and leadership

7. **Four Corners Native American Ministry**
   581254 - North America, United States, New Mexico
   Sharing God's love and reconciliation with the Navajo Nation via church growth and community outreach

8. **Mississippi Choctaw United Methodist Mission**
   761544 - North America, United States, Mississippi, Neshoba County
   Progressing towards health and wholeness and developing Choctaw leadership

9. **Native American Children's Fund**
   583581 - North America, United States, Oklahoma, Oklahoma City Providing school clothing, and helping small churches buy material for vacation Bible school

10. **Native American Comprehensive Plan**
    982615 - North America, United States, US Regional
    Provide leadership development to Native Americans within the UMC; work with existing congregations and help annual conferences to establish new churches; and bring Native American disciples into the forefront of ministry at all levels of the UMC.

11. **Navajo United Methodist Center**
    581535 - North America, United States, New Mexico, Farmington Providing transitional shelter for women and children of domestic violence and homelessness

12. **Nome Community Center Youth Programs**
    931610 - North America, United States, Alaska, Nome
    Providing an after school refuge offering quality, culturally relevant social service activities

13. **Nome United Methodist Church Sun Ministries Outreach Program**
    931602 - North America, United States, Alaska, Nome
    Repairing and winterizing facilities for Inupiaq and Siberian Yup'ik Eskimo community and volunteer

14. **Oklahoma Indian Missionary Conference Construction Project Fund**
    583633 - North America, United States, Oklahoma, Oklahoma City Constructing new church facilities and securing funds to assist Volunteer in Mission teams

15. Oklahoma Indian Missionary Conference Parish Partners
583634 - North America, United States, Oklahoma, Oklahoma City Freeing pastors to work without financial worries by paying them a full salary with health benefits

16. Rural Alaska Native Adult Distance Learning Program, Alaska Pacific University
3021099 - North America, United States, Alaska
Helping students financially who are majoring in education, human services and health administration

17. Southeastern Jurisdictional Agency for Native American Ministries
791842 - North America, United States, US Regional
Creating ministry awareness for unseen, overlooked populations while celebrating cultural heritage

18. Spirit Lake Ministry Center
3020453 - North America, United States, North Dakota
Assisting the children and elders through material help, building projects and vocational training

19. Tree of Life Ministry
123615 - North America, United States, South Dakota, Mission
Sharing faith through offering groceries, meals, home repairs and supporting language and culture